"Dr. Welch has carefully crafted realistic strategies for healing your marriage that will lead you to a new way of living and show you that transformation is possible. As a counselor of over thirty years, I highly recommend the solutions presented in this book. You will find new understandings and new answers."

—**Dr. Gregory L. Jantz, PhD,**
popular speaker, founder of The Center for Counseling & Health
Resources, and award-winning author of *Battles Men Face*

"In *The Controlling Husband: What Every Woman Needs to Know*, Ron Welch is a great diagnostician. He describes problems that will have many couples saying, "Yes, yes, that's us!" But where he shines is in his tried-and-true solutions in breaking the bonds of the controlling husband. His solutions—praising, finding hope in, forgiving, and serving *each other*—will create real mutuality in the one flesh of marriage. Highly recommended."

—**Everett L. Worthington Jr.,**
Author of *Moving Forward: Six Steps to Forgiving Yourself
and Breaking Free from the Past*

the controlling
husband

the controlling
husband

WHAT
EVERY
WOMAN
NEEDS
TO KNOW

DR. RON WELCH

Dr. Ron Welch was Associate Professor of Psychology, Colorado Christian University

Revell

a division of Baker Publishing Group
Grand Rapids, Michigan

© 2014 by Ronald D. Welch

Published by Revell
a division of Baker Publishing Group
P.O. Box 6287, Grand Rapids, MI 49516-6287
www.revellbooks.com

Printed in the United States of America

Library of Congress Cataloging-in-Publication Data
Welch, Ron, Dr.
    The controlling husband : what every woman needs to know / Dr. Ron
Welch.
        pages cm
    Includes bibliographical references.
    ISBN 978-0-8007-2230-2 (pbk.)
        1. Control (Psychology)—Religious aspects—Christianity. 2. Husbands—
Psychology. 3. Marriage—Religious aspects—Christianity. I. Title.
BV4597.53.C62W45 2014
248.8′435—dc23   2014001392

Unless otherwise indicated, Scripture quotations are from the Holy Bible, New International Version®. NIV®. Copyright © 1973, 1978, 1984, 2011 by Biblica, Inc.™ Used by permission of Zondervan. All rights reserved worldwide. www.zondervan.com.

Transformational Marriage™ is a trademark owned by Transformational Marriage, PLLC.

14 15 16 17 18 19 20   7 6 5 4 3 2 1

*To my wife and soul mate, Jan,
whose love, forgiveness, patience, selflessness,
and kindness have given me
the courage and motivation to become
the husband she so richly deserves*

Contents

Acknowledgments

First and foremost I want to give all the glory for this project to my Lord and Savior, Jesus Christ, without whom this means nothing. I want to thank my family for their unwavering love and support:

My wife, Jan, and our sons, Britton and Brevin, who have sacrificed immeasurably to allow me the time and space to complete this labor of love

My mom and dad, who sacrificed so much throughout their lives to provide a loving, Christian home for the children they loved so deeply

My sister, Cheryl, who has helped me see how narrow my perspective on the world has been and who has opened my eyes in so many ways

Jan's family (her sisters, Julie and Susan; her father, Harvey; her mother, Teal; and her stepmothers, Phyllis and Fredi), who have each played a part in helping her become the amazing woman that I am so fortunate to have married

This project would never have happened without the help of a group of people who believed in me and in the value of couples learning how to handle power and control in marriage:

Revell, a division of Baker Publishing Group, who took a chance on a new, unpublished author

My editor, Vicki Crumpton, who saw something in me and in this work that led her to invest the time and energy it takes to train and teach a new author

My agent, Greg Daniel, who believed in the project, agreed to represent me as a new author, and worked so hard to find a publisher for the project

Mary DeMuth, to whom I owe so much for helping me complete the original book proposal, without which there would be no book

Denver Seminary; my provost and dean, Randy MacFarland; and my division chair, Fred Gingrich, for providing the much needed sabbatical time to complete this project

I also want to thank the individuals who agreed to review early drafts of the book to help in the editing process: Abby Blacklock, who edited the early chapters and the book proposal, and Elsie Dodge, Cheryl Welch, and Julie Leathers, who reviewed the final manuscript before it was submitted.

I would be remiss if I didn't thank my clients from more than twenty years of practice who have opened their hearts and lives to me and whose stories have contributed so much to my understanding of marriage. In addition, I wish to thank the hundreds of students that I have taught over the years, along with my wonderful faculty colleagues at Denver Seminary, as their insights and wisdom are represented in these pages.

Last, and definitely not least, I want to thank my good friends Wayne Darbonne, Doug Dawson, Sharon Gipe, Jim Howard, and Danny McIntosh for their personal support and friendship during this long endeavor.

Introduction

Jan Welch

If you're holding this book, deep in your heart you are yearning for more in your relationship with your husband. Perhaps this was a gradual change or perhaps you suddenly woke up to the fact that your marriage is on a shaky foundation. You do remember the man you couldn't wait to marry, but the honeymoon is definitely over.

You may feel smothered and unable to make the simplest decision without his approval. You probably feel that nothing you do is ever good enough for him. You may have even given up hoping you could be the wife he wants. More often than you would like to admit, you ask yourself, *Is this the best my life can be?* You are clutching this book tightly in your hands, afraid to hope that you can still have the marriage you dreamed of. You don't want to rock the boat and make things worse.

How long have you been feeling this way? One year, five years, ten years or more? If I told you that it is never too late to rebuild the foundation of your marriage, would you believe me? You don't know the man who wrote this book, but I do. You may not trust him yet, because, well, he's a man. I think you will learn to trust him as you hear his story in this book. For now you can trust me, because I'm not just saying that I know how you feel—I've been there.

As you read this book, you will be walking in my shoes and discovering that we share a common experience of feeling powerless in our lives and marriages. The details of our stories may be different, but our desire to be empowered, to be heard, and to have a say in our lives ties us together.

I believed that when I said "I do" to the man of my dreams, everything would be wonderful—all the old hurts and disappointments from my childhood would be left behind. I quickly discovered that the baggage from our past, including my feelings of low self-esteem and Ron's anger and insecurity, had made the journey with us. Unfortunately, we were too naïve, too stubborn, and too proud to ask for help early in our marriage.

I felt alone and ashamed that I had allowed myself to become controlled in so many ways and given up my voice and my dreams in the process. Divorce was never an option for me, so I decided to make the best of the situation. I learned to live with the limitations on my life and found happiness in being a mom, but I knew my children would grow up and the emptiness would remain.

I should have been more honest with my husband. I should have told him things had to change, instead of settling for the status quo. Fortunately, Ron made the decision on his own to become a better husband and began to create change in our marriage. At first, I would not believe that he was serious. I was afraid to get my hopes up and be disappointed. That may be where you find yourself.

Looking back, I might not have believed myself if I had read what you are reading now, but there were no books around like this back then. I was afraid to believe that things could change—you'll read more about that in the coming pages. For now, you can find hope in the knowledge that you can learn from our story and not make the same mistakes.

I want you to know that you are not alone. You *can* have the marriage of your dreams. In fact, you have taken the first step by choosing to read this book. Change starts with believing that your husband can change and you can change. You can put aside the pain and frustration of the past and embrace the possibility of a true partnership in marriage. Take what you learn in this book, put it into practice in your marriage, and share this book with your husband. Together, you can find healing, hope, and love in your relationship.

Part One

Why You Can Believe Transformation Is Possible

Our Story

1

Why This Book Is for You

> Power doesn't corrupt people, people corrupt power.
>
> William Gaddis

I never wanted to be *that guy* . . . you know, the one who thinks the world revolves around him and lets everyone else know it, the man who always wants to be in charge and drives people nuts because he always thinks he's right. Somehow, without even realizing it was happening, I became *that guy*. I've heard all the names—control freak, egomaniac, narcissist, know-it-all, controlaholic (okay I made that last one up)—but you get the picture. For many years, I was the poster boy for controlling husbands.

I don't consider myself to be a particularly bad man and I don't believe I suffer from any specific mental illness. I can be narcissistic at times, I have problems with anger control, and I can be extremely selfish, but I'm not evil. What I have done is spend much of my marriage caring more about myself than my wife and children.

If you are in a controlling relationship, then the journey my wife, Jan, and I have been on can be helpful to you. We know what you are going through—we've been there. In this book I will share my own experiences and those of my wife, with the hope that our story will encourage you, empower you, and motivate you.

The good news we have to share with you is that *it doesn't have to be this way*. I am not the man I was, and our marriage is now so much closer to the relationship we always dreamed we could have. You can have hope because controlling husbands *can* change. There is no magic cure—we must work every day to make our marriage the best it can be—but there are clear steps that both husbands and wives can take to get out of the rut they are in.

If you have chosen to read this book, you have likely been in relationships with controlling people, are in one now, or see issues of power and control in yourself or those around you. This book is not a light read; it addresses heavy subjects, forces you to evaluate yourself and your marriage, and will likely make you want to do things differently. Your interest in this book means that you have a desire to change your relationship, help your spouse grow and change, and make changes yourself. If you are looking for solid, practical tips for this type of relationship transformation, then you have come to the right place.

Control and Power

It can happen in the car, at the ball game, in the grocery store, on the phone—you name the place—and if the conditions are right, you and the one you love can end up in a disagreement. It may start as a minor difference of opinion, and sometimes it ends right there. There are times, though, that the disagreement turns into an argument and the argument into a major conflict. Some of you can get into arguments that would make your mother (or at least your grandmother) blush. Others of you have perfected the silent treatment. Regardless of your technique, you are probably concerned about how conflict is being handled in your relationship.

Control and power in relationships are best seen on a continuum; they will be present in all relationships to some degree. Sometimes the power struggles are very small and easily resolved, while others can last for hours or even days. In a world of finite resources, there is no way we can have everything we want. There are times when negotiation is possible, but often one party (or both) has to give up some of what they want. If the power struggles are resolved well, through honest and direct communication, couples can move on and be no worse for wear. However, when resentment builds up and scorecards are kept, trouble is just around the corner.

Power comes in a variety of shapes and sizes. Some individuals use the frontal assault and knock down the door to get their way. Others come in the back door in a stealth attack. Still others utilize those around them to do their dirty work for them. Our selfish human nature leads us to want to have our way, but power is a finite resource—when you gain power, someone else loses power.

This was not what you signed up for, right? When you said, "I do," you didn't plan on all these conflicts and power struggles. But the desire to control our own destiny seems to be intrinsic in human nature. The problem with this is that we simply can't all have everything we want, and when needs overlap, conflict is sure to follow.

In my work as a psychologist, marriage therapist, and professor, many discussions center on power and control. I believe that you can learn from the experiences of other couples and that you do not need to make the same mistakes others have made. With experience comes wisdom, and with wisdom, transformation. I am living proof that change is possible, as I have personally experienced the power of the principles in this book and seen them change my marriage.

No matter where you find yourself in your relationship, take heart. You may be a wife who feels helpless to change her husband, believing, *That's just who he is.* You may be a husband who was given this book by your partner and you are reading it under protest and have to admit some of the concepts hit a bit too close to home. You may not currently be in a relationship because you lived through the pain of being controlled and now fear getting back on the horse and trusting a new partner. Even if you feel your marriage is going well, you will still find many suggestions that can strengthen your marriage as you understand how control and power dynamics play out between a husband and wife. This book is a testament to hope and transformation and the possibility of your marriage becoming what you have always dreamed it could be.

I should say up front that when I use the words, "I had a client . . . ," I hold my clients' trust in utmost confidence and respect and I would never reveal the identity of any individuals who have allowed me the privilege of hearing their story. So to that end, the stories that you read in this book will not contain any identifying information or any details that might give clues to a person's identity. To quote a well-known philosopher (Joe Friday of *Dragnet* fame), "The names [and the details] have been changed to protect the innocent."

Benefiting from This Book

Let's talk about who will benefit from reading this book.

First, it is written for those of you married to an arrogant, selfish man who cares primarily about himself or a narcissistic man who is trying to cope with feelings of insecurity. It is vital to understand what is happening in your marriage. If a man is married solely for what marriage does for him, then he may choose divorce over the opportunity to change, but then again, he may not. A narcissistic husband may consider an alternative way of living if he believes he can still protect himself in the process. In my experience, you find out whom you are really married to through a process of elimination—if he rejects all of the principles I suggest in this book when you try to incorporate them into your marriage, you may very well have your answer.

Second, this book is *not* written for those in a marriage in which violence is currently happening or is a real possibility. It is important to understand the difference between violent individuals who willingly injure their wives physically and insecure individuals who act in controlling ways out of anxiety and fear. Insecure individuals will use bravado to cover up their insecurity and they will control others, needing someone to depend on them. An insecure, narcissistic husband can learn a different way to meet his needs without hurting his wife. In stark contrast, a violent, sociopathic man will do whatever is necessary, including engaging in violence, to force his wife's compliance.

If you are married to a man who is violent in any way, you need to seek protection for yourself and professional interventions for both of you immediately. As a clinical psychologist, I know firsthand the trauma that confronting a violent individual can cause. If there are real risks of physical violence, you should not confront your spouse on your own. It is extremely important for the potentially violent individual to engage in an intense program of domestic violence intervention, while the other partner seeks individual counseling in a safe and protected place. Confrontation and healing can occur only after the potentially violent individual has learned to control his anger issues and there is safety in the relationship.

Third, this book *is* written for those of you who are overwhelmed by your husband's controlling behavior, those who are not sure that your husband can change, and those who don't know how to talk to your husband about his controlling behavior. In this book you will learn how to approach the subject of control with him, how to help him see the value in changing his controlling behavior, and how to believe that he is capable of change. You will learn how to choose the right time for these conversations, how to get around his resistance to the topic, and how to prevent the discussion from becoming confrontational. You will also learn how to set boundaries in your marriage and hold your husband accountable for transforming his behavior.

Fourth, this book *is* written for husbands who have received it from their wives, husbands who discover their wives are reading this book, and husbands who realize they tend to act in controlling ways. You may read many things you don't like or things that offend you, and some of what you read may hit too close to home. I know. I have been where you are. That is exactly the reason this book is perfect for you. You just have to keep an open mind and believe me when I say that change is possible. I've seen it happen in my life. I've seen it happen in the vast majority of men who have sought my help with their marriages. You might as well keep reading. What do you have to lose?

Fifth, this book *is* written *both* for those of you who have seen the role religion plays in encouraging controlling behavior by husbands *and* for those of you who have no religious faith system at this time. The core principles of Transformational Marriage, the term I use, are consistent with biblical teaching. I am a Christian and my faith will be evident throughout this book. However, the principles of power and control, as well as the suggestions offered for changing controlling behavior, will be beneficial and useful to all readers regardless of their faith tradition.

At the same time, it is important to note that this book *will* address the many ways in which churches and religion affect power and control issues in marriage. For instance, many husbands see passages in the Bible that address submission as giving free rein to husbands to exert control over their wives. The various understandings of submission, and their effect on how control issues play out in marital relationships, will be addressed in great depth.

Last, this book *is* written for spouses of controlling partners and the controlling partners, regardless of whether the man or woman is the most controlling. You may be in a relationship where the wife is the controlling spouse. If you are a wife and are also the more controlling person in the relationship, my comments to controlling husbands will be relevant to you. Trying to write to every potential type of relationship style is impossible. My high school English teacher always encouraged me to "write what I know," so I have chosen to do exactly that. I know what it's like to be a controlling husband and I know what my wife had to deal with being married to me. My experience may not be the same as yours but it can still be helpful to you.

The Source of Marital Conflict

You and your spouse don't wake up in the morning and say, "I think I'll get in a power struggle with my spouse today." Given the opportunity, you would probably choose a less hurtful, less stressful, and more loving marriage. However, you now find yourself in a place where your relationship does not feel the way you know it should. The good news is that there is hope for a new life through transformation in your relationship.

You may have gone to counseling to address these relationship issues and experienced some short-term gains. You may have even tried to "fireproof" your marriage, as the popular book *The Love Dare* suggests. Often these changes don't last, and the harsh reality is that many couples return to a life of anger, resentment, frustration, and unmet expectations. You may have even considered contacting an attorney, having concluded your marriage will never change.

Remember when you both said, "I do"? You made some important promises to each other. If you are reading this book, I'm guessing one or both of you have not kept some of those vows. How do two people who stood up in front of their family and friends and promised to love and cherish each other forever end up so angry and disappointed with each other? Husbands and wives say things to each other in frustration that they would never say to a stranger on the street. Promises are broken, and the loss of innocence and trust is collateral damage.

Some say it is all about anger, that one or both need to take anger management classes. On the surface, this seems to make a good deal of sense, because when anger gets out of control, it can be a frightening thing. Suppose that both of you controlled anger well—would your marriage problems be solved? I have worked with couples who don't get angry, at least externally, and still have significant marital conflict. I would argue that anger is only part of the problem, perhaps more of a symptom than a cause.

Others feel the big issue is communication. In their eyes, the main challenge these couples have is that they can't talk to each other, listen to each other, or understand each other. On balance, I can't argue with this logic. Learning to remain calm, talk about issues, and compromise helps, but I have seen couples who are masters at communicating that still have affairs, act selfishly, and abuse alcohol and drugs. Like anger, poor communication causes difficulties in a marriage but may be more of a symptom than the source of the problem.

There are those who blame marital problems on society and the current breakdown of the nuclear family. Their explanation for the conflicts we experience is that many of us did not have good examples of how to handle conflict when we were growing up. According to government statistics,[1] the divorce rate continues to hover around 45 to 50 percent, indicating that many children don't have the best role models for conflict resolution. Current societal trends seem to indicate a movement away from a traditional nuclear family rather than toward it. Even if this might change sometime in the future, you can't wait to solve the problems you have in your marriage right now.

A Different Explanation

Anger control, communication, and role models in the family of origin are all important factors that influence how couples handle conflict. I have come to believe, however, that these influences are best described as either secondary causes or symptoms of a much deeper issue. There is a stronger driving force that creates conflict in marriage.

The Destructive Power of Selfishness— "It's All about Me!"

I believe that selfishness, and the resulting desire for power and control, is the single most powerful force operating in controlling relationships. Sometimes it is a small decision, such as which restaurant to eat at or what color to paint the walls in your home. Other times the decisions have massive consequences, like whether to have another child or take a job in a new city, for example. Regardless of the size or shape of the issue, a decision has to be made, which will be impacted by whose voice is louder and whether both parties will compromise or fight to get their own needs met. If one gives in this time, who will give in next time—and will the one who gives in resent what he or she lost?

Willard F. Harley, Jr., in *Effective Marriage Counseling*, talks about his Love Bank concept. He notes that in marriage, "Neither should gain love units at the expense of the other's account. Control in marriage does the opposite. Instead of making simultaneous Love Bank deposits, control can cause simultaneous withdrawals."[2] He describes progressive stages of controlling behavior, including selfish demands, disrespectful judgments, and angry outbursts. He calls these behaviors "Love Busters" that interfere with trust, intimacy, and love in the marriage.

In today's narcissistic, "It's all about me" world, most people talk about wanting to get their needs met in a relationship as opposed to meeting the needs of their partner. Jean Twenge, the author of *Generation Me* and coauthor of *The Narcissism Epidemic: Living in the Age of Entitlement*, studied sixteen thousand university students and discovered that 30 percent of them met the criteria for narcissism, as compared with only 15 percent in 1982.[3] Across the board, people strive to achieve control of circumstances in their lives and of their relationships. From the extensive testing involved in relationship websites like Match.com and eHarmony. com to the plethora of relationship books out there, "experts" trumpet the theme of finding that one person who will meet your needs. The expectation is that we are in relationships to get what we want and need from the other person.

The Constructive Power of Selflessness— "It's All about You!"

Throughout this book, you will hear me voice a different idea— one that conflicts directly with what society says we should look for in relationships. I want to suggest a different model that focuses on how you can serve the other person instead of on what you can get from her or him. The selfless model is not new or unique to me—in fact it has its roots in the biblical model of servanthood from the Christian faith tradition. This model of marriage is based on selflessness rather than selfishness—taking care of your partner's needs before you worry about your own.

I can already see the emails coming in: "Are you kidding me, Welch? It's already all about him—why on earth would I want to sign up for this? What about me? How do I get my needs met?" Fair point—if you give and he takes, how do you survive?

My answer is this: two people looking out for themselves are actually less powerful than two partners looking out for each other. I realize this may sound like a fantasy in light of your current relationship, but it is the goal we are aiming for. I encourage you to look for small victories that show movement toward that goal.

Controlling husbands can learn how to value their wives over themselves, giving them priority. This involves baby steps for husbands who have been taught to "look out for number one" first. Wives will need to help their husbands learn to make changes in their daily thought processes and actions that will make selflessness a new way of life.

Hope for Wives

I have a friend who asked me what possible reason a woman could have for staying married to a man who controls her. In my friend's words, that is "just plain stupid." I do not believe that wives of controlling husbands are intellectually challenged, so perhaps you remain in a controlling relationship because you don't feel you can leave or because you receive some sort of benefit from your relationship. I am going to suggest throughout this book that you may have a lot more ability to control your relationship than you think you do. I am even going to suggest that power and control in relationships is a two-way street, with both parties participating in the process.

Perhaps your husband treats you well when he is not angry, aggressive, or domineering. Perhaps you feel that being unhappily married is better than being divorced and alone, as you fear loneliness most of all. Or maybe you have never known another way of being in relationship, as you have been controlled before and this feels familiar and comfortable despite the pain. Each of you knows your own heart and knows why you remain in a destructive relationship.

Our story, and those of the couples I have worked with, will provide you with the hope that it doesn't have to be this way. There is a path that can lead to a marriage in which you feel valued, honored, heard, and loved. Your husband is not doomed to be the man you see before you now. With the right motivation and desire, he can become the man you have always hoped he would be.

The good news is that if you were married to a man who simply couldn't care less about you and had no desire to be with you, you would likely already be divorced. But since you are still married, there is hope for change. It will not be easy; he will not change overnight. For now, just understand that there is another option besides the divorce behind Door #1 and the unhappy marriage behind Door #2. If you both are willing to put in the time and energy, Door #3 holds the potential for a transformed marriage.

Hope for Husbands

To husbands, let me say this. When I decided to write this book, people told me you wouldn't read it. They said that wives would read the book because they have to live with you, but you wouldn't pick it up. So kudos to you for looking for a better way to live.

Maybe your wife gave you this book. Maybe you are thinking about someone you know (the "I have a friend who . . ." phenomenon). Regardless of why you are reading this book, you will probably see some controlling traits in yourself. Maybe you make decisions based mainly on what you want. Perhaps you get too angry at times and you can be a scary guy. When it comes down to it, you have to admit that often you care more about what you want than what your wife needs.

It took a lot of guts to pick up this book and give it a chance. I know people say, "I know how you feel" too often, and they usually don't. In this case, though, you can believe me when I say, "I understand what you are going through." I can honestly say that I have been where you are (or at least someplace close).

If you live by any kind of moral code that says controlling the one you love is wrong, your behavior creates a problem for you. You have to either convince yourself you are not doing anything wrong or live with the contradiction between your thoughts and actions. Some of the things I say in this book may hit close to home, and I can promise you that I will probably offend you more than once. Do yourself a favor and just keep reading. The truth may hurt when you first hear it but it will also set you free.

You can take heart in the knowledge that you can change. There's a better way. If you keep reading, you will learn how. Don't settle for the status quo. Your wife deserves better; you deserve better.

Beginning the Process

I don't believe it is an accident that this book has found you at this time in your life. You, as a wife of a controlling husband, are ready for a change but you may not think your partner wants to change. Some of the principles in this book don't require your partner's cooperation—you can begin the process of change on your own.

In later chapters you will learn how to change your expectation that he will fail, how to set appropriate boundaries and hold him accountable for his behavior, and how to initiate conversations with him about these difficult issues. Other steps will require that both of you work together for lasting transformation.

First, I want to tell you the story of transformation in my marriage. My wife and I hope this will be blessing to you. Telling our story leaves us feeling vulnerable and exposed but we have chosen to do this in the hope that you can learn from our mistakes and gain encouragement from our successes. Every couple's story is unique, and yours is different from ours, but we are glad you are allowing us to share this journey with you.

2

How I Became a Controlling Husband

> What is love? Love is when one person knows all of your secrets
> . . . your deepest, darkest, most dreadful secrets, which no one
> else in the world knows . . . and yet in the end, that one person
> does not think any less of you; even if the rest of the world does.
>
> Unknown Source

I didn't wake up one morning and say, "I think I'll be a controlling husband." It was a slow process that began innocently enough. I learned patterns from my parents that were problematic, but many of my most positive personality characteristics also come from them.

I grew up in the little farm town of Caldwell, Idaho. We lived out in the country, and I spent the summers working in the cornfields. I did well in school and was active in our local church. I didn't have many close friends—I was overweight, the "smart kid," and the "church kid" and not one of the "popular kids."

My dad was a God-fearing, honest, hardworking man who taught me solid moral ethics and set high expectations. He always managed to attend my school and sports events, and we always went to church on Sundays. He loved my mother deeply and remained faithful to her throughout their marriage, taking care of her and providing for her until the day he died. He did have some difficulty with anger and stress that would be formative in my life.

My mom was a beautiful soul who loved my father with all her heart. She was a model of Christian servanthood, a truly gifted listener, and a selfless person. She taught me to forgive quickly and permanently, to listen well, and to enjoy the small things in life. She wasn't perfect, and her tendency to worry excessively rubbed off on me as I grew up. I never doubted that my mom and dad loved me, and they were always there for me. Our family doesn't have any deep, dark secret that excuses or explains my behavior.

Baggage

Isn't it amazing how much unknown baggage we bring with us into our marriages? Hindsight is 20/20, and in retrospect, I believe that the baggage I brought with me into my marriage caused significant problems. Our baggage is incredibly hard to get rid of; no matter how many times we think we have it secured in the overhead bin, it keeps falling out. We realize that we are replaying tapes from the past, but they are programmed into us so deeply that it takes a lot more than mind over matter to change our thinking and actions.

I hear comments like these from my clients all the time: "I didn't sign up for this." "If I had known he would get this jealous, I never would have married him." "Just how much do I have to put up with? This is ridiculous!" Yet in almost every case, there is more than enough baggage to go around on both sides, despite what the partner who is protesting the loudest says. Clients may say they understand that "he got it from his father" or "the apple didn't fall far from the tree." However, understanding is not enough to alleviate the resentment they feel.

I learned to be anxious from my mom. While benefiting from all her wonderful qualities, still I grew up knowing that she was constantly worrying and fretting. From her perspective, the glass was not only half empty, it was draining rapidly. My mom could think of every possible negative event that could happen and would worry about every single one. I never understood how she could have such a strong faith in God and seem to be so secure in what she believed but not trust God to protect her from the things she worried about.

Apparently she recognized this as a problem and didn't want to pass it on to me. She even bought me my own personal "worry wart." I still have it in my office. It's an ugly thing that is supposed to represent your worries and remind you not to worry about everything. If I had learned to use it, I might have been a lot better off. As it was, I kept focusing on what could go wrong in my life, rather than expecting things to go right. I got pretty good at it too.

As I describe the specific coping skills that I learned from my parents, think about your own childhood and adolescence. What baggage did you bring along from your youth that affects your marriage today? Try to identify at least three tendencies that you brought to the marriage that create difficulty in your relationship. Ask yourself if you are spending more time criticizing your partner for his baggage than you are dealing with your own.

While reading our story, it may seem that some things in our relationship were much worse than in yours, while other parts of our story may seem mild compared to what you experience. Control and power in relationships are always a matter of degree.

The Creation of a Controller

Anxiety: Bad Things Can Be Prevented

I believe that anxiety and depression are like a staircase—you work really hard climbing up the stairs trying to prevent something bad from happening (anxiety) and then you slide down the stairs really fast toward the bottom when you realize you can't prevent all bad things from happening (depression). This helps explain why controllers work so hard to control everything around them.

Most controlling men spend a lot of time driven by the fear that something bad will happen to them if they don't take steps to prevent it. For some, it is because they felt out of control as a child and never want to feel that way again. Others lost something or someone dear to them and want to do everything possible to prevent that from happening again.

I spent much of my life as one of those guys. If it was at all possible, and it often was, I would do whatever was within my power to prevent a bad thing from happening. I had the intelligence to figure out strategies for preventing these bad events and the persistence to make the strategies work. A lot of controlling men live in this fear-driven, anxious reality.

At some point, bad things happen anyway. We either don't or can't do enough to prevent such things. Car accidents happen no matter how safely you drive. People die no matter how much you love them or try to protect them. The belief that we can prevent all bad things from happening is purely a fantasy, but if a man delays or interferes with enough negative events, he can begin to believe he can influence things that are really in God's realm.

Anger: It's Easy

I came into my marriage with a much larger anger-control problem than I realized and I think this was due to a combination of genetics and learned behavior. I learned so many good things from my father, including my work ethic, my standard of excellence, and my devotion to local church ministry. However, he also taught me how to get angry.

I don't know about any of you, but when I heard my dad shout my middle name, I knew it wasn't going to be pretty. My dad didn't always seem to have a clear reason for being angry. Sometimes, I think I was just around at the wrong time and was the most convenient target. Sometimes he would yell—sometimes he would spank. I can still remember the pink yardstick (yep, it was pink) that hung in the broom closet in the dining room.

I remember getting pretty angry myself but I don't recall this causing me difficulty until I started dating. When romantic adolescent feelings were combined with anger and jealousy, then control became a problem. It became so much easier to get angry than to deal with my emotions.

What frustrates me, looking back now, is that most of my anger as an adult has been either misplaced or completely unnecessary. I get mad about the most insignificant and irrelevant things. For years I let sports teams have way too much influence in my life. People refused to watch games with me because I was no fun to be around. I missed out on many opportunities for fellowship by being more concerned about the score than about the people I was with.

For me, anger is a default option. When something upsets me and I feel insecure or uncomfortable, the easiest way to respond is to get angry. Sometimes it was something small, like a young child making noise in the pew behind me in church or a meal that wasn't prepared exactly right at a restaurant. I became a perfectionist who wasn't satisfied with anything.

Now I realize if things really do go wrong, my angry response is a matter of choice. I can blame someone else for the problem (anger) or blame myself for the problem (personal responsibility). It's easier to blame someone else. I know that sounds selfish, but that's the point. It takes a lot less work to blame someone else.

I don't think I'm the only guy who thinks this way. I have seen many of my friends, fellow coaches, colleagues, and clients behave in the same way. You have to work much harder to stay calm and think of other people when you are frustrated. It takes much less effort to simply be angry and assume anything that goes wrong is someone else's fault.

Insecurity: Bad Things Can't Always Be Prevented

Once we fail in our attempts to prevent bad things, we feel as though we're heading down a flight of stairs. In fact it begins to feel as if the stairs are a slippery, downhill slide of helplessness and frustration. As long as we feel we can do something about the bad thing, we still have hope and we keep taking action. When we begin to feel the bad thing will happen no matter what we do, we start feeling depressed and stop trying to do anything. From that point on, insecurity sets in, and we just wait for the bad things.

The last part of the puzzle for me was a strong feeling of insecurity in relationships with women. I didn't feel insecure in other areas, as I was successful in school, in music, in athletics, and in leadership in my church and service organizations. For me, the insecurity was focused on what girls, and later women, thought of me. I was overweight when I was younger, until I lost a tremendous amount of weight in my first year of college. My self-esteem with the opposite sex was not strong, and when I did find the courage to ask a girl out, I was often turned down.

I have seen this in others as well. A corporate executive who is completely confident in his ability to manage a huge corporation may be extremely insecure when it comes to his relationship with his wife, causing him to wonder if she is having an affair. A professional athlete may have no question about his ability to perform on the field yet worry constantly about his ability to be a good husband and father.

When I did have relationships with girls in high school, they betrayed me in various ways several times. This meant that I had trouble trusting new relationships and became quite gun-shy. My anger and anxiety combined with my insecurity and created my first steps into controlling behavior in a relationship.

In college I began a series of relationships in which, for the first time, I began to try to prevent betrayal from happening. I became jealous, controlling, hypervigilant, and overbearing. The relationships didn't last long. Once the women realized how I was treating them, they quickly disengaged. Some of them tried to confront me, while others just left, but I did not learn from these experiences. By the time I met Jan, I had become convinced that I needed to maintain as much control as possible in a relationship to prevent things from going wrong. I wanted to be loved but I couldn't trust that a relationship could last.

My experiences in relationships really represent the anxiety-depression staircase. I had been burned before, so the pain of betrayal, rejection, and eventual abandonment was the thing I feared the most. I did everything in my power to try to prevent these events, but my behavior only increased their likelihood. Like the proverbial bird in a gilded cage, the love I was hoping would grow was crushed by the weight of my jealousy and control. To protect myself, with the alternative being depression and helplessness, I would often become even more controlling, being too fearful to trust the other person, let alone God.

Why This Should Give You Hope

My controlling behavior may not sound exactly like that of your husband, but probably there are elements that match. I believe these three factors of anxiety, anger, and insecurity are not unique to me. I think they are keys to understanding why men control their wives. Most of the bravado and dominance in the controlling husband's behavior is due to the underlying insecurity and fear for which he is compensating.

This fear was strong enough that even though I saw the destruction my controlling behavior was causing in my wife and my children, I convinced myself the alternative was even worse. I'm not asking you to understand my thought processes, as I realize they aren't logical. I do hope I can help you see inside the mind of a controlling husband. I was not then, nor am I now, a bad person. I was, and still can be, so scared of being out of control that I maintained the fantasy that I could somehow prevent bad things from happening if I just controlled those around me tightly enough.

This can give you hope, whether you are married to a controlling husband or you are one yourself. When a husband understands the reasons he acts the way he does, the chances of his changing and becoming the husband he is capable of being are greatly increased. In this book you will find the knowledge and skills you need for transforming your marriage, just like we did.

3

The Care and Feeding of a Controlling Relationship

My wife will tell you that she saw the warning signs even before we got married but she overlooked them. These included choices I made to prioritize my own needs over hers, decisions that reflected my thoughts and desires more than hers, and discussions that began with an issue she brought up and somehow transitioned to talking about my concerns.

She came into our marriage expecting that it would be different from what she had known as a child. She wanted our marriage to be a relationship in which she would be valued, honored, and respected. In her words, "Sometimes the only way I could endure my childhood was to dream about my future and the man I would marry. Maybe someone would love me for myself and not try to make me something I was not or make me feel unworthy because of my faults. It was wishful thinking, but when you struggle to discover who you are because you have spent your life trying to be what others want you to be, you just want to be loved for who you are."

Jan tells me that she had been looking forward to our wedding day for her entire life. She had always believed that when she started life with the man of her dreams, she would be saved, leaving her past behind. Perhaps "Prince Charming" is a bit too strong a term, but she definitely did feel that I swept her off her feet. She was so ready to be loved unconditionally, to have the kind of love she had read about as a young girl. Even more important, she had been certain that I was the man for her, the man for whom God had been preparing her all her life. She truly believed that I was "the one."

Of course, I wasn't perfect, and some of her friends and family had made comments. "Are you sure you know what you are doing?" they would ask. "How well do you really know him?" She would smile and assure them that there was no need to worry. "He's everything I've ever wanted in a man. I am so lucky to be marrying such an awesome guy." She didn't think much about their concerns; they didn't know her future husband like she did.

She told herself: *Okay, so he does get a bit jealous at times. Doesn't every future husband feel that way about his fiancée? What I really want is to be cared for, valued, and loved. He really seems to love me, and if I have to put up with a bit of jealousy, that isn't too much of a price to pay, is it?*

You Got Married *How* Fast?

I met Jan at the University of Denver in 1986, while I was in my senior year and Jan was taking classes in the master of arts in communication program. We both enrolled in a class in interpersonal communication. Our professor warned us that every time he taught this course, two students met, dated, and got married. We laughed that off, not knowing what was to follow.

Unbeknownst to me, Jan had been watching me during the course. She had been interested in how I interacted with others and the comments I made in class. Honestly, I was not watching anyone in the course; I was just trying to finish my degree.

I'm the kind of guy who not only has to-do lists but has color-coded to-do lists. And I had made a thorough list of the qualities I was looking for in a wife. I know, where's the romance in that? Save that thought, and we'll see if you think I'm a romantic in a few minutes.

This class had numerous assignments that were conducted with a partner in the course. Usually I did those with my best friend, but one night, I ended up doing an exercise with Jan. As the exercise went on, Jan started flirting with me, and I started marking points down on a sheet of paper each time she did. She was sweet, endearing, and very attractive, and I found myself instantly attracted to her. When the class ended, I told her that I felt she needed to do something about those points she had built up and I could be convinced to wipe out the points if she would have dinner with me. She didn't hesitate, saying she would love to go out for dinner.

Here's where I start to look really bad. I asked Jan if she had a quarter. She said, "Sure!" Then I used the quarter to make a call (yes, that was in the dark ages when we used pay phones). The line was busy, so I hung up and we sat down on a bench to wait until I could try to call again.

Jan asked whom I was calling. In retrospect, this was an opportunity for me to avoid the official title of "jerk" in the narrative. However, I actually told her, "I'm calling the girl I have a date with on Saturday night to reschedule so I can fit you in." Had I been a more sensitive guy, I would certainly have been more tactful. To this day, I thank God that the line was busy. As I explained to Jan my intention to call this other young lady and ask her to a movie that evening, she lifted her head slowly, batted her eyelashes in a manner that I still feel was purely angelic, and whispered, "I like movies."

The arrow Cupid shot went straight to my heart. We went to the movie (*Young Sherlock Holmes* for those of you who like details) and we have been together ever since. We talked throughout that night and spent the next few evenings together talking about long-term plans. Jan cooked dinner for me on our third evening together, and when she walked out in the most amazing black dress I have ever seen, any last remnant of common sense I had washed away. I asked Jan to marry me in the lobby of the Stanley Hotel in Estes Park, Colorado, only five days after our first date. On our sixth day together we were looking at wedding rings. We were married four months later. True love is an amazing thing.

Surprised by Anger

Even in our short engagement, there were warning signs of my jealousy and anger that Jan ignored. For instance, we were each driving our own cars across town to the same location one night, and Jan thought it would be fun to race and see who got there first. When she beat me (let's just say that back then she viewed speed limits more as recommendations than laws), it made me very angry. Other than my pride being hurt and my not being in control of the situation, there was no reason for me to have been upset. Jan recalls being rather stunned by the depth of my anger and frustration.

Another early warning sign was the way I reacted to her friendships with other guys. I was extremely jealous, based on my insecurity and the expectation that she would leave me for someone else. You know the old adage that love is like a butterfly—let it go free and, if it returns to you, it was meant to be? I clearly did *not* subscribe to that theory. I held the belief that if you watched the thing you loved closely enough, you could protect it and prevent it from flying away. I told myself that I wanted to protect Jan from harm, but I really just wanted to protect myself from abandonment.

If you are not a controlling person, you probably don't understand that logic, but that's how we controlling folks live our lives. If you do nothing to try to prevent bad things from happening, you are completely helpless. If you do everything in your power to prevent the bad thing you expect, then maybe—just maybe—the bad thing won't happen. Looking in the rearview mirror, I can see how disrespectful and selfish my jealousy was. It pushed Jan farther away when I wanted to bring her closer.

Power and Control in Our Marriage

Jan believes that from the beginning of our relationship she allowed me to have control. She grew up as a people pleaser and found it easier to let others have their way if it made them happy. She worried that, if she made a decision and I didn't agree with it, I would get angry or quiet or punish her in some way. This was where the dance got started for us. I was used to getting my way, and Jan would almost always choose to do what I wanted so I would not be angry. She would rather be unhappy than endure my anger. Jan would tell you that, for her, this was easier. She was used to being unhappy or depressed.

Jan's father was a very controlling man and was used to getting his way. He also had a pretty strong temper. It is possible that her dad acted this way out of insecurity, as I do. I never asked him, so I don't know, but I do know that Jan ended up being attracted to a man who had qualities similar to those of her father. Recently she told me that she never saw this similarity until well after we were married. Looking back, I would say she was blinded by her desire to be loved and married and to get away from her past. There were many warning signs that things might not turn out well, if she had looked for them.

Control is not evil by nature. Without some degree of control, chaos would ensue. To function properly society requires some shared standards. Imagine roads with no stop signs or streetlights;

think of countries with no laws or rules. So too in marriage, a complete lack of control would make it unlikely that the relationship would be effective, productive, or rewarding to either party.

Decisions require an element of negotiation. Someone is likely to get more or less of what he or she wants in most situations. The question for couples is who gets what when, how positive or negative the negotiation process becomes, and whose feelings get hurt during the discussion. Sometimes it comes down to which partner is most affected by the decision or who cares the most about the issue.

Jan and I have had many of these conflicts over the years, and we handle, or perhaps more accurately *I* handle, these disagreements much better now than I used to. At times Jan has felt caught between a rock and a hard place. She has to decide the importance of fighting for a certain issue and sometimes decides, "It's not worth the fight."

Some situations are important enough for her to take a stand and let me know how much something means to her. For example, as a teacher at a small private school, Jan is very involved in the lives of her students, and they often invite her to their extracurricular activities, which she enjoys attending. In the past, I would have been offended if such a request interfered with my plans. But now I honestly feel better when my wife tells me how much she wants to attend an activity, and we arrange our schedules to be sure she can go.

Installing the *Kindness Filter*

Because she came from a family where she had no voice, sticking up for herself has been hard for Jan. In contrast, stating my opinion has never been a challenge for me. In fact I tend to say more than others want to hear.

People tell me that I should have been a lawyer, as arguing comes so naturally to me. I have a gift (or a curse, depending on your point of view) for being able to persuade people. My wife tells me that it often saves time and energy to let me have my way. Do you know anyone like that? Annoying, aren't we?

My wife swears that, early in our marriage, we would have a discussion and she would begin with a very clear point of view. But after talking with me for a while, she would find herself agreeing to a viewpoint that was diametrically opposed to where she started! Honestly, I don't recall having entered these discussions with the intent of changing her mind or "winning" the argument. Nonetheless, it is clear I was mainly focused on my own needs.

I have installed what I call a *kindness filter* on myself. I stop and intentionally consider whether a potential comment is necessary, whether it will hurt Jan's feelings, and whether it will make the experience more enjoyable and relational for us. The first step in this process is training yourself to say absolutely nothing at first. The second step is to evaluate what you intend to say. Be sure that your words will be kind and sensitive. Stop—evaluate—then speak. Once you train yourself not to verbalize every thought you have, you have a lot more time to consider what you will say and the way it will affect your spouse.

Thanks to Jan's feedback and my desire to change, I have become much better at filtering what I say. I have to be careful when something frustrates me, and I still forget to filter my words and actions through the kindness filter at times. I have discovered that just as my controlling behavior reinforced itself, thinking about what I say and the effect it has on Jan is also reinforcing; the more I do it, the easier it gets.

An Opportunity Missed

When Jan was growing up, her family rarely, if ever, went to church. She attended Catholic school, but her memories of this seem to be more focused on fear of the nuns' discipline than Christian ethics and principles. When we got married and she saw the faith I described and wanted to share with her, she was very open to it. I had the opportunity then to show her the love, acceptance, forgiveness, and salvation that I cherish so much in my Christian faith. One of my deepest regrets is that I squandered this opportunity.

From an early point in our marriage, I was extremely jealous, overtly controlling, and subtly manipulative in a variety of ways. I overreacted to innocent interactions that her bubbly personality led her into, wanted her to do most everything my way, and used anger and domineering responses to control her. So, unfortunately, I was showing her a confusing mix of church on Sunday morning and manipulation and control Sunday afternoon through Saturday. My hypocrisy led her to question the value of the faith I said I believed in.

But even in the darker years of our marriage, most of our friends would not have known the challenges we faced. We were both good at hiding them, as I expect you are. I was very devoted to the needs of others in my work and did my best to meet my supervisor's expectations. We attended church as a family, the kids were involved in youth groups, and I served on leadership boards, as well as playing keyboard and singing with worship teams. However, a pattern started to emerge in which Jan tried to predict my reactions and avoid any behavior that would provoke a negative response from me. She could have set much stronger boundaries and refused to allow me to control her, and now she feels she allowed this unacceptable behavior from me for far too long.

I am thankful that throughout our marriage we have been active church members and Jan shares my faith in Christ. Finally, in recent years, my behavior has been more consistent with my faith. I hope that as I continue to grow and change as a husband and father, and as a Christian, she is seeing the image of Christ now that I should have shown her all along.

Looking Forward

Many times over the years I have talked with both my sons about how my behavior affected them. My older son, Brit, tended to respond with anger of his own in response to my attempts to control him, as he is a strong individual with some of the same qualities I have. This has helped him be an outstanding leader, a talented engineer, a strong husband, and a man of principle and honor.

However, just as I had to overcome the double-edged sword of these traits, I believe he will have a challenge as a husband and a father to overcome these traits as well. He will have to be aware of the risk that his anger could get the best of him and realize that his intelligence and strong beliefs will need to be tempered by compassion and willingness to listen to others.

Brit didn't appear to have any difficulty standing up to me and refusing to allow me to control him but he did resent the times in his teens when I enforced control. Now it's interesting that he tells me he thinks I am too hard on myself and that I wasn't as bad a father as I feel I was.

In contrast, my younger son, Brev, is a much more sensitive soul. He is an outstanding athlete and performs at high levels for his coaches. However he is much more like Jan in his personality style, tending to internalize feelings of hurt and anger, rather than expressing them, and he takes the words I say very personally. When, over the years, I have gotten mad or acted in controlling ways, he has found it very difficult to deal with emotionally.

Recently Brev told me that he wanted me to know how hard it is for both him and his mother when I respond in angry, controlling ways. "You say words that you can't take back, Dad. Sure, you apologize and say you're sorry. But you can't take the words back. They hurt really bad and it takes a long time to get over them. Just so you know, Dad, Mom feels the same way. We're a lot alike, and you have to be more careful with the words you use." He is wise beyond his years, and all of us with controlling tendencies would do well to listen to his advice. He certainly has my attention.

Brev's comments reminded me how much my past behavior continues to cause difficulty, even after I have worked hard to change what I say and do. When you have been a controller for a long time, the people around you come to expect it. It makes me sad that people I know have said to themselves, *That's just Ron. That's just who he is.*

The challenge this creates is that once people begin to see you a certain way, they expect you to behave that way. I can't blame my wife, my sons, or my friends and colleagues for expecting that from me—I created that expectation. However, for things to change in the family system, everyone has to start looking forward rather than backward. If you want to increase the likelihood your husband can and will change, you have to start expecting him to succeed in these changes. Believing in him will increase the chances that he will believe in himself.

Living in the past is a recipe for maintaining the patterns that have gotten you where you are today. Living in the future unlocks the possibility that things can be different. I tell my clients that focusing on the past can lead one to feel depressed and defeated, but focusing on the future creates hope, anticipation, and belief in the possibility of change. It is my sincere desire that you, and your family, accept the invitation to look ahead with hope to a new and brighter future, rather than looking over your shoulder toward the past.

Part Two

Why He
Controls You

Understanding Your
Controlling Husband

4

The Alpha Male Problem

At a certain point, even if the one alpha male is dominant, at a certain point there's a younger lion that is stronger, and everyone knows it.

Josh Lucas

Men have a lot in common with wolves. They mark their territory, they strut in front of the female of the species, and they bristle at the presence of another alpha wolf. We learn this behavior from older wolves, who are more than happy to train us. These older wolves take the shape of coaches, fathers, teachers, older brothers, and eventually bosses at our jobs. The world of men seems to revolve around this spirit of competition and the principle of survival of the fittest.

In the wild, only the strongest survive. For a pack of wolves to survive and prosper, they must be stronger, smarter, faster, and braver than all the other packs. Such a pack requires direction, plans, structure, hierarchy, and discipline. In short, this type of pack requires a leader. Enter the alpha wolf.

David Mech popularized the concept of an alpha wolf, although he has most recently reported that this concept may relate more to breeding than physical domination.[1] Regardless, the alpha wolf concept, whether completely understood or not, describes a wolf who strengthens his dominance in the pack through intimidation, power, and control. This concept is relevant to understanding controlling husbands.

Development of the Alpha Male

Vince Lombardi, the legendary Green Bay Packers coach, said, "Leaders are made, they are not born. They are made by hard effort, which is the price all of us must pay to achieve any goal that is worthwhile."[2] I believe that the formation of an alpha male husband begins at a very early age and continues in stages. He is molded through experiences that range from the kindergarten sandbox to youth sports to father-son interactions to the work world. Exploring the developmental stages that form alpha males will help you understand the formation of a controlling husband.

The Sandbox: Arena of Competition

Young boys learn competitive and controlling behavior at an early age. Take the sandbox, for instance. A young boy enters this den of competition either as an only child who has had all his toys to himself or as a child with siblings with whom he has learned to fight for the toys he wants. One child enters the sandbox with no knowledge of competition, having had his way in the world. The other enters with his battle skills honed in family competition.

Young Johnny, an only child of two loving parents, enters the playground for the first time. He has no idea that there is any such thing as competition, as his parents have always doted on him and he has had free rein with all of his toys at home. He brings two of his favorite toys with him and begins playing joyfully in the sandbox.

Already in the arena is little Bobby, a sandbox veteran, who has had several experiences with other children and is displaying a dominant personality style. He tends to want to get his way and is usually able to do so. Bobby sees the cool dump truck that Johnny brought with him and wants to play with it. He walks up to Johnny, takes the dump truck, and starts driving it. Johnny is upset but doesn't understand what happened. He wants his truck back, goes over to get it, and Bobby gives him the "try and take it back" look that has served him well in the sandbox. Johnny reaches for the truck; Bobby pulls it away and says, "Mine!" and the competition has begun.

At this point in the sandbox experience, alpha males begin to be formed. Johnny has three options. He can back off, give up on his toy, and allow the dominant male to win, resulting in the loss of his possession and an image of himself as weak and subservient. Or he can choose to fight, become physically aggressive, and attempt to take the toy back, finding out if he is able to dominate Bobby physically.

His third option is to use his intelligence, which can be just as powerful as physical control, and find ways to manipulate the situation to get his toy back. Regardless of the approach Johnny takes, he will learn from the consequences of his choices. If he wins the battle, through his intelligence or his physical strength, he will feel the intoxicating sense of power and control and will have developed a skill set that he is likely to use again. If this pattern is repeated and reinforced, the formation of an alpha male is underway.

Fathers and Sons

I remember vividly the images of my dad's frustration when something broke or a plan got messed up when I was a young boy. It would happen in an instant, as his frustration turned to anger, often aimed at me for something I had done wrong. When my father was angry, everyone knew it, and the family turned its attention to him until the issue could be resolved or punishment for the offense had been handed down. Things weren't okay in the family until Dad calmed down. This was a foreshadowing of things to come in my future marriage and family.

I didn't know it at the time, but I was getting my first lessons in how to handle power and control. When something went wrong, anger was a way of achieving a feeling of power over a seemingly out-of-control situation. I remember numerous times when Dad would come home from work late, tired and frustrated. All I had to do was ask a difficult question or state my view on something that we disagreed on, and he would respond in anger, making me feel as if I had caused his frustration, whether I had or not.

At other times, Dad would refuse to accept the situation and use whatever influence he had to try to change things. If we were eating out and the food was not to his liking, he would be visibly upset and the entire dinner conversation would be disrupted. He would stare at the waitress, make repeated comments about the establishment, and generally make everyone miserable until the situation was resolved. Often he would not let the issue go even when the dinner was over, making a point of tipping less or talking about the fact that he would never come back to that place.

Sons watch their fathers like hawks and learn the good and the bad from them. Fathers, if they are in their sons' lives, are the strongest and most effective male role model they have. Like little sponges, boys soak up all they are shown and learn a great deal about how to treat women from watching their dad. It is a responsibility that fathers should not take lightly.

Coach Obvious

Both my sons have had outstanding coaches as well as very destructive coaches in their years in sports. They have played for win-at-all-costs coaches who yelled at them and benched them if they didn't play well, but they have also played for coaches who loved them and built them up no matter how they played. The effect a coach can have on a young man's confidence cannot be underestimated.

My younger son has had the privilege of being coached by Justin Olson for many years. Justin is always positive, so much so that I have sometimes scheduled a baseball lesson with him to help Brev when he was struggling in school. I knew my son would spend an hour with Justin and come out of the lesson beaming with pride and confidence in who he was, and this would lead to better performance in school. Justin has taught Brev to relax and not worry about the outcome of his play, to focus on the effort he puts in, and to be satisfied with doing his best. Justin has had such a positive effect on the man Brevin is becoming.

Coach Rod Olson (no relation) is another such coach for whom my son has had the privilege of playing. Known to his players as Coach O, Rod is the author of the new book *The Legacy Builder*.[3] Coach O refers to many of the coaches he has seen as Coach Obvious. These are the guys who shout from the bench the whole game and make brilliant observations like, "Hey, Andrew, keep your eye on the ball." *What do you think he's trying to do, Coach? Watch TV while he's batting?* Coach Obvious will say, "Ben, what are you doing? Run faster!" *Sure, Coach. He's trying to run slower and let himself be tackled. That will really impress his teammates.* And then there is my personal favorite, "Come on, Johnny. Throw strikes." *Like he's throwing balls on purpose, Coach? Really?*

This type of coaching helps explain why so many kids drop out of sports at an early age. A report from the Institute for the Study of Youth Sports[4] indicates that this type of coaching contributes to a vast number of young athletes quitting sports altogether. Most important, many of the athletes cited negative coaching and unreasonable expectations as the factors that led them to quit. From an early age, young athletes are pushed so hard that they no longer enjoy the sports they used to love.

This developmental rite of passage we call youth sports is extremely important in understanding why husbands control their wives. The experiences men have in athletics are set against the backdrop of feedback from their fathers. In fact, they often interact with each other, as a father may try to vicariously relive his failed athletic career through pushing little Billy far beyond his abilities.

This is the reason ten-year-old baseball players are playing eighty to one hundred games in a summer, twelve-year-old football players practice five times each week with games on Saturdays, and fourteen-year-old athletes have reconstructive shoulder surgery from throwing 120 pitches every game. These boys are driven by coaches who yell and degrade them, believing they are actually helping them play better. When their parents join in this win-at-all-costs mentality, the results can be disastrous.

Succeeding in the Work World

In the work world, power equals control. When you have power, you can determine much more of what happens to you and your family. Power equals money; power equals prestige; power equals time. Perhaps most important, power means that you are not powerless. When you have power in your job or career, others can't tell you what to do—at least not as much. The most intoxicating thing about having power in the work world may be that you do not experience the absence of power.

Alpha males gravitate toward positions in the work world that provide the type of control they enjoy. They become the officers in the military, not the enlisted soldiers. They become the managers in business, not the employees. For many, the cutthroat nature of their jobs causes them to need to *eat or be eaten* and this reinforces patterns of intimidation, manipulation, and control. Those who win the battle at work end up stepping on some toes to get where they want to go, rationalizing that their behavior is okay because they are doing it for their family.

Men who lose the battle to be dominant at work often take on the alpha male role at home, where dominance is easier to attain. And men who are successful alpha males at work find it hard not to allow alpha male behavior to affect their marriages when they come home, even though at home they are expected to stop giving orders, stop directing others, and stop being in charge. The military and law enforcement husbands I have met tell me this is especially challenging for them.

Many controlling husbands can't make this shift from controlling others at work to not controlling family members at home. In the work world they are trained to use others to get their work needs met. In the world of their family, however, they are expected to be kind and think of other family members before themselves. For alpha males to become loving, caring husbands who prioritize their families above themselves, this problem has to be addressed.

Living with an Alpha Male

As a woman, there can be times when you feel good about being in a relationship with an alpha male. In fact his confidence and leadership may be aspects of his personality that attracted you to him in the first place. There are fringe benefits provided by being married to an alpha male. It can be good to have a man around who deals with things, takes care of unpleasant tasks, and perhaps even takes the blame when things don't go well. He's pretty good in a crisis, and you can usually depend on him to take care of you.

The question is, at what cost? If he is always running the show, where do you fit in? How do you earn his trust and show him that he can depend on you also? As time goes by, something happens to your self-respect. A part of you begins to say, *It's just easier to let him take charge. Why should I bother? He's not going to listen to me, anyway.* This is the beginning of what psychologists call "learned helplessness." We'll talk a bit more about that later, but suffice it to say that when you've been knocked down enough, it doesn't take a rocket scientist to realize it may be smarter to quit trying to get up.

As I've said, there are many good qualities about the alpha male. The challenge is for him to find a way to maximize the ones that enhance a marriage and minimize those that don't. What would convince an alpha male he needs to change and meet this challenge?

Alcoholics talk about "hitting bottom," so maybe the alpha male needs to lose enough things he values to be convinced of the need for change.

If he is still putting himself first, he has not yet hit bottom. He probably doesn't even know what the *bottom* looks like. He hasn't lost his wife, he hasn't lost his kids, and he probably still has a job and a home. He still does not understand what his wife is going through, he doesn't understand how his behavior is inconsistent with the promises he made, and he doesn't understand what a poor example he is for his children. So what would encourage him to change? He has what he wants, is able to control the relationship, gets the power and stability he craves, and does not pay any price for his controlling behavior.

Transforming the Alpha Male

Don't be fooled by the intimidating exterior of the alpha male. Sometimes his bark is truly worse than his bite. You may be tempted to believe that he can't change, but the beauty of the alpha male is that the very qualities that make him control you are the ones that can help him change. Most alpha males are intelligent, resourceful, resilient, and relational. These are all qualities that can help them change the behaviors that cause difficulty for you.

There are really three areas that the alpha male has to address if he is to channel the positive aspects of his personality into becoming the husband you need him to be. He has to learn to trust the leadership skills of others, to transform competition in relationships into cooperation, and to prioritize others' needs over his own. Let's take a look at how he can do this in your marriage, and how you can help.

1. Trust Other's Leadership Skills

If an alpha male wants to become a better husband, he first has to consider that there might be a better path than the one he is on. He has always been in charge—in groups, in relationships, in school, or at work. That's how he likes it. However, there is an underlying belief that fuels his desire to be in charge. He believes that he will not, or cannot, be content if others are in charge. The feeling of being out of control is something he avoids at all costs.

If he is to change, he has to learn to let others, including his wife, take the wheel and trust that the ship will still get where it needs to go. Alpha males don't have to give up being involved in decisions or become subservient members of the pack. They can simply learn that all members of the pack have value and others have leadership qualities that, at times, are even better than their own. The alpha male husband needs to learn that true leadership often consists of helping a team develop to the point that they function extremely well on their own without direct guidance. The best leaders are those whose organizations function seamlessly when they are not present.

You can help your husband learn this valuable lesson by deciding to stop letting him take over and to set some boundaries. Choose some situations in which you feel you have knowledge or experience that has prepared you well for leading your family in these areas. Suggest to him that although you value his leadership, both of you need to be able to share the load and take responsibility. Talk with him about how he can help you feel respected and valued in the marriage by trusting you.

2. Transform Competition into Cooperation

Another step in this transformation is for the alpha male to begin to consider that first is not always best. He has always looked at life as a win/lose proposition. The idea of winning through cooperation might have been presented by coaches or teachers, if he was lucky, but the primary message he internalized was that winning was the goal.

Whether it is an argument with you or a sales competition at work, it's always been about being number one, regardless of who gets hurt along the way. When you have a discussion, he looks at the disagreement as an opportunity to prove his point, similar to a lawyer in a courtroom. In fact, he may only hear a small portion of what you say, as he is too focused on preparing his counterargument.

You can improve the likelihood that he can change this trait by helping him see that marriage is not about competition. Ask him how he likes it when you prove a point to him or embarrass him by telling him when he's wrong. Ask him to consider not correcting you every time he has a different opinion but instead to agree to disagree. Do you both have to have the same opinions on everything? Of course not. That only happens because he believes he has to force you to come around to his way of thinking.

You can have a tremendous impact in this area by modeling the type of behavior you would like to see from him. When a difference of opinion occurs, don't start the conversation by proving your point or simply quitting because it's not worth the fight. Start by letting him know you'd like to talk about the issue and that it is okay if you end up with different opinions. Suggest that the best outcome is for both of you to feel closer as a couple and for each person's ideas to be valued.

3. Turn Self-Focus into Focus on Others

The last element of change in this area involves the alpha male learning to think of others before himself. Alpha males can become husbands who honor, respect, and love their wives, but they cannot do this if they continue to assume that they are the center of the world. The alpha male husband absolutely must begin to see himself as only one part of a family system. This will be difficult for a man who has generally thought of himself first for most of his life.

However, the good news is that this step becomes much easier when it comes after the first two steps we just discussed. As an alpha male husband begins to trust others more and realizes he doesn't have to do everything himself, he instinctively begins to understand that the family system works better as a team. As he begins to interact with you in more of a cooperative way than by competing with you, he learns to see things from your point of view. This sets the stage for this final change in perspective.

You can help complete this transformation by talking with him about the value you see in the qualities that his alpha male character includes. For instance, you could let him know that his ability to figure out ways to solve problems is a strength that you depend on, while telling him how much you value his resilience and intelligence. There is no reason he has to feel that these qualities are inherently evil—he simply has to see how they can result in harm to the relationship if not kept in check.

These changes won't occur overnight. I would encourage you to begin working with him on trusting you more in areas of the marriage that may be less threatening to him. Move into helping him see that you are not the enemy that he has to defeat, but a teammate that can be of great benefit to him if he will work with you. Don't settle for giving up or letting him have his way because it is easier. Stand your ground, set boundaries, and help him see that he can learn to value your needs and desires over his own. The key is to help him use the very qualities of his alpha maleness that have created difficulty to create transformation in truly positive ways.

5

The Three Keys to Control

I don't care what you think unless it is about me.

Kurt Cobain

There are three unique aspects to the personality of a controlling husband—intimidation, narcissism, and selfishness. Keep an open mind as you read about these three concepts. My definitions and explanations of how these things operate in a controlling husband may be much different than the traditional definitions.

This chapter will help you understand a controlling husband behind the scenes, much like drawing back the curtain to see the true Wizard of Oz. The experiences you have had and the emotions you feel may make it hard to catch a different vision for what drives your husband to act like he does. It is my belief that controlling husbands present a mixture of intimidation (through anger and manipulation), narcissism (an egotistical presentation that covers up underlying insecurity), and selfishness (caring more about his own thoughts and feelings than his wife's). These very characteristics are also the reason you can believe in his ability to change, as each of them can be overcome.

Key 1: Control through Intimidation

Lord Acton, in an 1887 letter to Bishop Mandell Creighton, said, "Power tends to corrupt, and absolute power corrupts absolutely." Power and control patterns in a relationship develop slowly over time, and the longer a difference in power exists in a relationship, the more noticeable that difference becomes. Power differences are bound to exist, and in a healthy marriage these ebb and flow and are shared with respect and dignity. In an unhealthy marriage, controlling husbands experience power and translate this into dominance through intimidation. In turn, intimidation can lead to exploitation and manipulation, resulting in fear, avoidance, and distrust in the relationship.

In many relationships there is a power differential, as in parent and child, boss and employee, teacher and student, military officer and enlisted person, police officer and civilian. In these relationships one person is meant to have more power so that the daily functioning of the family, the school, or society will go smoothly. Problems can develop, however, when power is exerted in inappropriate ways—a teacher gives an undeserved low grade, a police officer arrests an innocent person, a parent grounds his or her child without cause. Sometimes just the threat of using power becomes intimidating and forces the less powerful person to comply.

Is there a power differential in your marriage? When I ask couples I work with this question, I get a variety of answers. Some couples idealistically respond that they are completely equal, while others can immediately identify who has the final say. Some couples report they trade off being in charge. However, when we talk about these issues in more depth, most couples are able to identify one partner who uses intimidating actions more than the other. Intimidating actions include raising one's voice, threatening consequences such as divorce, or talking over the other person.

If you perceive that you have less power, you have likely had thoughts like these: *I wish he would quit talking over me. Why doesn't he care about what I say? He thinks he's always right, and it's just not worth it to argue with him.*

For most couples, there is a real power differential in their relationship, with one partner being more controlling than the other. When one partner thinks that the other is more controlling and intimidating, it is what I call an *unspoken truth* in the relationship. I will discuss this in more depth in chapter 17, "Serving Each Other." For now, suffice it to say, they are unwritten rules that govern the relationship and are accepted by both partners.

In his book *Why Does He Do That?* Lundy Bancroft describes the words women in relationships with controlling men use to describe them:

He's two different people. I feel like I'm living with Dr. Jekyll and Mr. Hyde.

Everyone else thinks he's great. I don't know what it is about me that sets him off.

I feel like he's never happy with anything I do.

He's scared me a few times, but he never touches the children. He's a great father.

He calls me disgusting names, and then an hour later he wants sex. I don't get it.[1]

Does any of this sound familiar? For many women, these statements describe what living with a controlling husband is like.

The Threat of Violence

Power differences in relationships, especially those involving intimidation, don't develop overnight. Letting small, seemingly harmless controlling behaviors go unaddressed can lay the groundwork for more direct aggression. Think back to the most intense arguments you have had with your spouse and ask yourself some questions: Were you afraid he might go to the next level? Has he raised his voice? Gotten in your face? Yelled? Punched a wall? Many times, the power that an intimidating person wields is due to the threat of physical violence.

The rates of intimate partner violence in our society are well documented. A large National Institute of Justice study reported that 7.7 percent of women surveyed reported being sexually assaulted by a current or former intimate partner at some point in their life. In addition, 22.1 percent of women and 7.4 percent of men surveyed reported that a current or former intimate partner had physically assaulted them at some point in their life. This same study noted that about 1.3 million women and 835,000 men are physically assaulted by an intimate partner annually in the United States.[2]

These violent interactions create an unwritten rule in the relationship that says, If you make me really angry, I will get violent. While physically abusive husbands actually use violence toward their wives, in any marriage, just the threat of violence creates the gradual power and control shift in a relationship. Harsh words can turn into more violent expressions of anger, ranging from threatening looks to yelling to hitting a table or punching a wall.

Confronting your spouse when he has shown evidence of potentially violent behavior is never a good idea. It makes sense to find a safe place to discuss this unacceptable behavior, such as with a counselor, pastor, or mutual friend, where it can be suggested that he have further counseling or attend anger management programs.

Other Types of Intimidation

Perhaps your husband has never used physical intimidation. There are many different ways of intimidating a person in a relationship without physical violence. Here are just a few of the examples I have heard in my practice:

- withholding sex
- blocking the door to prevent the partner from leaving the room

- threatening to go away with the kids
- threatening divorce
- threatening suicide or self-injury
- withholding access to money
- revealing relationship secrets to others

The list could go on and on.

Verbal abuse can be just as intimidating as anything physical. Marital verbal abuse consists of negative, critical, and hurtful statements that are demeaning and contemptuous. Gary Chapman, in *Desperate Marriages*, notes, "We are now coming to understand that verbal abuse can be fully as devastating as physical abuse. Verbal abuse destroys respect, trust, admiration, and intimacy—all key ingredients of a healthy marriage."[3]

The Development of Intimidation

Anger can appear to explode in an instant, raging like a forest fire. A recent Colorado forest fire that destroyed thousands of acres of beautiful forest and many homes started with the calm embers of a fire pit. Even in this instance, however, the warning signs existed. Smoldering embers, white hot and ready to combust, were ignored for days. In marriage this lack of attention to small, seemingly unimportant incidents can turn minor sparks into marital infernos.

It is quite compelling to follow the development of controlling, intimidating behavior. Small decisions that an individual makes over the course of time as he observes the world around him build a personality that needs to be in control. It can start in childhood when a young boy watches his father get what he wants by telling his mother what to do. Or it can start in the classroom when boys find the teacher calls on them more often than on girls, giving them a sense of superiority. Maybe these ideas get reinforced when boys enter the sports arena and learn that threats of power, violence, and strength lead to victory and success. Then they can apply the skill sets they've learned to their relationships with women, which encourages them to view women as objects.

One client told me that he watched carefully when his parents argued. His mother would say something, and his father would respond by raising his voice, pounding his fist on the table, and standing up in an intimidating fashion. Magically his mother would become quiet, and his father would get his way. This taught the client how to win an argument.

In adolescence this man discovered that his father's pattern of intimidation worked quite well during disagreements. When he began dating, he learned to demand what he wanted, and generally women responded in compliant ways. For this man, the practice of power and control came full circle, being passed from father to son, and he became the same man his father had been.

Gary Chapman gives us an inside look into characteristics of the power that controlling spouses hold. Jodie, a wife he describes in the book, reported that her husband "controls the money like he is a guard at Fort Knox. I have to ask for every nickel. . . . He wants to know everywhere I've been and what I've done. . . . I feel like I am a bird in a cage . . . actually . . . a hamster in a cage—I don't have wings anymore."[4] This is often the outcome when the imbalance of power happens gradually. Chapman believes that the husband's need for control stems from either his childhood upbringing or a long-term personality style issue.

Unbridled verbal abuse can lead to violence when revenge distorts our perspective on relationships. Gary and Carrie Oliver, in *The Complete Marriage Book*,[5] shed additional light on this topic. The Olivers note that most married couples view anger as an inherently bad thing that can be used to buy a wife's compliance. Whether his anger is covering an underlying resentment or a suppressed hurt, the outer expression of it is often verbal and/or physical abuse.

Society has a tendency to assume that controlling men are mean, vile creatures who need to be mocked and avoided. Some current authors such as Dorothy McCoy in her book *The Manipulative Man*, do exactly that.[6] Her first chapter title, "Manipulation—Thy Name is Man," is derogatory enough, but she quickly resorts to blatant insults, comparing manipulative men to Charles Manson, Stalin, and even Hitler. McCoy's claims that controlling men need to be "housetrained" and that the purpose of her book is to provide women with "a garlic necklace, silver bullet, and wolfsbane to protect you from the manipulators who would selfishly use you" are not helpful. In contrast, my intention in this book is to provide a constructive and useful method of understanding verbal abuse and intimidation in controlling men and how they can change.

Key 2: Control through Narcissism

When you think of a narcissist, you probably think of people who are egotistical, big-headed, know-it-all, and conceited. However, despite popular belief, the mental health field now defines narcissistic people differently. They are more accurately described as selfish. Truly narcissistic men are better characterized as scared little boys who are so deeply insecure that they project a false persona of competence and control to the world around them. If you are married to a narcissist, you already know this because you feel like you have another child to take care of instead of a husband to share your life. My wife understands well the needs of a "high-maintenance husband."

Narcissistic husbands differ from intimidating husbands in that they would rather have their insecurity needs met without hurting their wives in the process, especially if they have a Christian or other moral ethic. This is precisely what makes them open to therapy and transformation. However, when these men who strive to maintain the image of control and power at all costs get challenged, they can respond with controlling behavior.

Living with a narcissistic husband might look something like this:

Lisa brought up a relatively harmless subject: the landscaping of their yard. "I was thinking about adding some roses in the back flower bed."

Mario raised his eyebrow and quietly said, "You think so? Really? I mean, I have spent hours trying to make the backyard look great, but it clearly isn't good enough. But roses would never grow in that flower bed."

Lisa knew where this was going, so she tried to stroke his ego a bit and said, "I'm not saying the yard doesn't look good. It looks great. I just thought roses would be nice."

Mario raised his tone of voice a bit and said, "Didn't you just hear me say that roses won't grow back there?"

Lisa regretted it the minute she asked the question: "How do you know they won't grow?"

Mario stood up, began to walk out of the room, and with a parting shot, said, "Fine. Plant your roses. Just don't blame me when they die."

Notice that in this example, Mario doesn't come off as violent or intimidating. Instead, his egotistical response becomes defiant and dismissive. He doesn't have to threaten or manipulate, as he simply disregards his wife's desires and feelings completely. This is how intimacy dies in relationships with controlling husbands. If the directly intimidating behavior doesn't kill trust and safety, the lack of respect and empowerment certainly do.

Narcissism versus Selfishness

Narcissism is a different type of control from selfishness. Selfishness is truly self-interest for its own sake. When I act selfishly, I want what I want, and the effects on others are simply collateral damage. Narcissism, in contrast, is a way of coping, a means of survival. When I act narcissistically, I am presenting an image to others, trying to appear more competent than I believe myself to be. I would rather not hurt those around me, especially those I love, but I don't know any other way to protect myself. This is why, in my opinion, it is easier to overcome narcissistic control issues than it is to deal with selfishness. Narcissists can learn another way to feel safe in the situation without harming the people they love in the process.

My controlling behavior starts with narcissism. I feel scared, jealous, or worried, and I want those bad feelings to go away. Acting out of self-protection, I use controlling behavior to reestablish feelings of security and safety. It's like grabbing a handhold when a bus turns sharply; I reach for something to stabilize my emotions. Unfortunately, Jan is often the one who feels the effects of my actions.

I think this is how it is for most controlling husbands. We don't really intend to harm anyone and we aren't purposely trying to meet our needs at the expense of our wives. The honorable and selfless thing to do would be to accept the feeling of insecurity and deal with the anxiety that it creates. But often this is when selfishness comes in, and we make a clear choice to prioritize our own needs and emotions over those of our wives.

The best time to intervene in this process is at the onset of feelings of anxiety, before they become overwhelming. I have found that I am much more effective in choosing to be selfless and thinking of Jan before myself when the emotions have not yet reached this point. The longer I wait, the harder it is to overcome the growing anxiety.

As the feelings of insecurity build up, however, the consequences of responding to them become ever greater, and I am less and less able to make the selfless choice. If you will allow me to revise an old phrase, rather than discretion being the better part of valor, selfishness becomes the better part of cowardice. If I wait too long in the process, I will choose to sacrifice my wife's needs to meet my own.

Key 3: Control through Selfishness

In addition to using intimidation and being narcissistic, controlling husbands maintain a self-centered approach to relationships.

They concern themselves more with what their relationships can give them than how they can meet others' needs. This selfishness drives their thoughts and behaviors.

For example, consider these "date night" scenarios: A selfless husband asks his wife what she wants to do for their night out and does everything possible to make sure it happens. But the selfish husband asks his wife what she wants to do, while actually thinking, *I really want to see that new action flick.* He begins manipulating the conversation to convince her to do what he wants to do.

You may be thinking, *My spouse isn't* that *bad.* If you are asking how good or bad your husband is, you are asking the wrong question. Instead, you should be asking, Why? Why does he act in selfish ways? When a selfish, controlling husband asks his wife what she would like to do, he doesn't actually want to know. Rather, he's initiating a game that he and his wife know he will eventually win. To maintain his self-protective image of the loving, caring husband, he asks for her input and indicates that he wants to know what she wants to do. In reality, he will listen to what she suggests, respond quickly with reasons why that would not work well (unless it is the same thing he wants), and then manipulate the conversation until they decide to do what he wanted from the start.

Selfishness versus Antisocial Behavior

In this book we are focusing on controlling men and not violent men. Though some of you may be married to a violent man who is also controlling, the vast majority of controlling husbands choose not to use violence if they know how to avoid it. Violent men, however, choose antisocial behavior because it seems like the best way to handle a situation. Husbands who control their wives out of a selfish desire to meet their own needs do not generally enjoy the chaos they create around them; they simply don't know any other way.

A truly antisocial man who uses his wife to meet his own needs has no interest in changing. The only change he would consider would be to increase the level of violence to intimidate his wife more or simply file for divorce.

The men I am referring to in this book are not always happy with their behavior and would consider an alternative if they could learn (1) a different way to be heard than through intimidation, (2) a better way to feel safe and secure than through narcissistic behavior, and (3) how to think of others before themselves. Until they see these possibilities, though, they simply deny the reality of their own behavior, using one of a hundred excuses for why they act as they do.

The Root of Control

Controlling, domineering behavior is a powerful addiction. The controlling husband may not experience a physical craving or withdrawal symptoms like a heroin addict, but power and control are as seductive and devious as any substance known to man.

Selfishness may be the most important key to understanding controlling husbands. The addiction's power lies in its ability to meet the selfish need. Take away the selfish desire, and you take away the need for the addiction. If a man can learn to be selfless, rather than selfish, controlling behavior loses its addictive power. Understanding this one truth is crucial to understanding why controlling behavior occurs and how to change it.

Patricia Evans, in her book *Controlling People*,[7] refers to correspondence she had with a couple of men who made a list of the ways they had been taught to control women. Here are just a few of the forty or so behaviors these two gentlemen came up with: Use relentless logic to argue, talk over them, talk to other men about women in dehumanizing ways, use men's privileged voice to interrupt, use public humiliation, pretend to be hurt when they question my behavior, listen in a preoccupied way, persuade her that she's too needy, and praise yourself by telling her you have never physically hit her.

Every single one of these behaviors is rooted in selfishness— evidence of husbands who place themselves above their wives. These behaviors occur on a daily, if not hourly, basis in controlling marriages. To change this pattern, the selfishness that pervades the relationship *must* be transformed into servanthood. This is the subject of chapter 17.

A Final Thought

This pattern of intimidating with anger and manipulation, creating a competent exterior to cover underlying insecurity, and being strongly self-focused, is not new. Controlling husbands have developed this personality style over a lifetime. Rome wasn't built in a day, and it won't be transformed in a day.

Please know that you can believe change is possible. I can testify to that. Don't give in to the thought that your relationship can't change—that your husband can't change. As we continue to unveil the reasons behind his behavior, you will also learn more and more about how he can change. Once you understand him better, we can move on to the principles of Transformational Marriage that you can use to transform your marriage, and you will see more clearly how to set boundaries, hold him accountable, and work together to help him become the husband you deserve.

6

The Three Questions
Wives Ask Most

When a man is wrapped up in himself, he makes a pretty small package.

John Ruskin

Question 1: Why Does He Overreact?

There's an edge in his voice—a *tone* that speaks volumes without his saying anything. It can happen in an instant or it can build slowly over a period of days. You never really know how bad it will be, do you? Sometimes he doesn't react at all to things you are certain will upset him. Other things that seem so small can set him off. You just hope it doesn't happen when others are around. It's so embarrassing.

Wives are always asking me why their husbands get so upset over little things, let alone big things. I have heard all sorts of complaints: "He ruined dinner because he had to point out the steak was overcooked." "His team lost and he was impossible to live with." "He just had to tell me how right he was." "He blew up at the kids over such a little thing." "He asked for my opinion, and I told him, and then he got upset and did what he wanted anyway!" You can't always see it coming but sometimes you can feel when the storm clouds are building. Why does he have to be this way? This is *not* the person you married!

I Have to Fix It

So, why do men overreact? In my experience, men generally overreact more out of a sense of helplessness than anything else. Something happens—maybe the remote control for the TV gets lost (you know that a man will move heaven and earth to find the clicker, right?). Of course, he will usually blame everyone else in the home before he considers that he might be the one who lost it.

If an issue develops that a man doesn't know how to solve, he takes it personally. He's supposed to be able to fix things; it's in his DNA. When something happens that he can't fix, he gets concerned and eventually becomes desperate. He begins to question his abilities and feels his manhood is threatened.

This is when he begins to overreact. It's a kind of defensive reaction to avoid the feeling of utter helplessness. If he can yell or swear or punch something, at least he's taking action and is not helpless. Sometimes just finding someone to blame, other than himself, makes things better. I know that makes absolutely no sense to most women. Often men feel better, at least for the moment, if they can just express their frustration in some way, even if in the end it makes things worse.

Actually many of these men regret what they are saying or doing when they overreact. In fact, only minutes later, a man may actually walk up to his wife, kiss her, and say something like, "Sorry I got upset, hon. I feel much better now." This drives women absolutely crazy. To him, it's over and he's moving on. The words he said and his actions may have created a firestorm in his wife's world, but he acts as if nothing happened at all.

Generally men don't overreact with any intention of inflicting harm. More often than not, it is much more of a response to a feeling of helplessness created by an unsolvable problem they are facing. This is not an excuse, although you may hear it that way. It is an explanation to help you understand why this happens rather than a justification for inappropriate behavior.

The Role of Anxiety

When people begin to be aware of something bad that might happen, they start climbing up the staircase of anxiety. Even if they tend not to worry about things, they still would like to prevent bad things from happening. Those who do tend to worry about things may even start running up the stairs.

This is the reason most of us take precautions to protect us against bad things. For example, if you are a student and you have a test coming up, you may feel anxious about the outcome. You assume the more you study, the more likely it is you won't fail, so to protect against failure and to reduce your anxiety, you study for hours. Maybe you have a teenage daughter, and you are worried that something bad will happen to her. Attempting to decrease your level of anxiety, you set up all sorts of rules concerning whom and when she can date. You truly believe that whatever you are doing will decrease the likelihood that bad things will happen.

We like to think that we are in control of our lives. But when something bad happens, like a tsunami or hurricane, our confidence in our ability to control things is shaken. When planes flew into the twin towers of the World Trade Center on 9/11, many people were confronted with the fact that they were not in control. As a result crowds of new people started attending church, praying, and talking about belief in a God who is in control. But according to the Barna Group,[1] less than a year later when things calmed down, we began to feel in control again and church attendance went right back down to pre-9/11 levels. Seems like many people want to believe in God when they need him but are quick to return to self-reliance when they don't.

The Big Lie Exposed

In truth, so much of what we believe is under our control is really not. We tell ourselves this Big Lie to convince ourselves that the world is a safer, less random place. At some point in our lives, we face situations that we can do absolutely nothing about. We accept the reality that the events we fear will or won't happen and that we have no control over the outcome. In either case, this is when we start back down the staircase toward depression, as the Big Lie is revealed for what it truly is.

I have seen this happen with clients who have been assaulted and will no longer leave their homes, fearing they will never be safe again. I once met a young woman who had been independent, outgoing, and confident in almost every area of her life. She went to public places on her own for years and never thought twice about it, until the day she walked out to her car and her world was shattered in an instant. A man followed her to her car, threatened her with a knife, sexually assaulted her, and then left her there.

When I met her, years after the assault, she still avoided any place that reminded her of the place where she had been assaulted. The police never found the assailant, and even though she had seen a counselor for a while, it hadn't helped. As we talked, she explained that her belief in a world that was safe and that she could control what happened to her was destroyed by this one incident. Her perception of the world around her changed.

For many of us a traumatic experience like a car accident or the loss of a loved one exposes the Big Lie. For me, it was the death of my father when I was in my thirties and the death of my mother ten years later. These events had a devastating impact on my understanding of God and the world around me. My childhood and early adulthood had been so sheltered that I had no concept of what real trauma or devastation was. Praying for so long that my father, and then my mother, would be okay and losing them both so much earlier than I had expected made me question my faith and where God was in the whole process.

Choosing How to React

While I was in Cambodia and Thailand recently, I found out how far I have come in handling situations when I am not in control. In the past, I have become quite anxious in such circumstances. At one point during this trip, we were crossing the border between Cambodia and Thailand. To do this, we left the van we were traveling in to switch to a different van on the other side of the border. We gave our luggage to a man with a wooden cart who promised to give it back in a few hours. At the same time, we gave up our passports to a couple of other individuals who, for a fee, promised to expedite our crossing to minimize the hours of waiting in lines that most people had to endure.

I found myself in a no-man's-land between Cambodia and Thailand, with no passport and no luggage! Knowing the difficulty losing your passport can cause in a foreign country, my anxiety was rising. The old Ron would have been very tense, argued that we shouldn't give up our passports, tried to figure out some other solution, and generally made everyone around me miserable.

However, in this situation, I actually found it was quite freeing to simply not worry about something I couldn't control. My traveling companions knew this was not my usual MO and gave me high fives when I turned over my passport! I don't know if I would have remained calm if we had lost the luggage and/or the passports (everything turned out fine), but my experience can give you hope that controlling men can learn to be comfortable being out of control.

So, Men Overreact Because . . .

Men overreact because they tend to expect they should fix the problem. This may not be what you want, but it's what they know how to do. When they can't fix it, and fix it fast, they become anxious and frustrated and react emotionally. In truth, men have way less control over what happens in their lives than they think they do. Understanding that this is the Big Lie they tell themselves is the key to overcoming this tendency to overreact.

Question 2: Why Does He Always Have to Be Right?

The other question that I hear repeatedly from wives of controlling husbands involves the husband's need to be right. "Why does he have to be right all the time?" "I can't remember the last time I shared my opinion, and he didn't give his in return." "He always has to make a comment on what I say, instead of just agreeing and supporting me." We all know how frustrating a know-it-all can be. Wives just want their husbands to validate what they say and respect them in the process.

Gender Differences

Throughout history it has been generally agreed that men and women are different. That idea is not so widely accepted today. In an effort to defend gender equality, gender differences are often discounted. Folks can be easily offended at the idea that men and women have inherent, perhaps genetic, differences. A recent 2012 study by Bobbi Carothers and Harry Reis, "Men and Women Are from Earth: Examining the Latent Structure of Gender,"[2] concludes that few differences exist. These researchers studied more than 120 traits in more than 13,000 people and concluded that men and women did not differ significantly in the character traits studied.

However, I believe there are a couple of important ways in which men and women are different. First, in my experience, men have less natural ability to adapt to new situations, while women are more flexible and open to change. Men seem to struggle more with midlife transitions, schedule changes, and unexpected challenges, while women balance careers and the unpredictability of child rearing and relationships every day. It does seem that women are intrinsically better able to adapt and flex with the changing realities of life.

Second, and perhaps more important, I believe men may have less ability to accept their own limitations, including their own mortality. Throughout my life and practice, I have observed that women are more apt to accept the harsh realities of life and to be more realistic and resilient in the face of tragedy. Often men attempt to fix or change the situation immediately, and if that fails, they deny that the problem exists. Men are experts at rationalization and denial, and if given the chance, can explain away almost anything.

Finally, it seems to me that men have more of a desire than women to be right, to win the argument, and to prove themselves effective. As with any observation, there are exceptions. Some women are just as determined to prove their worth through winning the battle or the argument. But in general, I believe men are more competitive than women.

Not Knowing How to Be Wrong

It may be that men have to be right because they don't know how to be wrong. Many men live their lives avoiding the reality that they have significantly less control over their lives than they think they have. If you doubt this, look at how men deal with tragedies, such as the loss of a child, often shoving emotions deep inside themselves. This explanation may be the most accurate and shed the most light on why men feel such a need to be right.

My mom did her best to teach me to accept that I could not always be right. On her refrigerator for many years, up until the day she died, was a small sticky note in my writing with the words,

"I was wrong, Mom. You were right." She believed it was worth the time and effort to teach me that I wasn't right about everything and that, even if I was right, I didn't need to tell everybody about it. Unfortunately, I'm still learning this lesson. I have had to write the same confession to my wife because I still struggle with wanting to be right.

A husband's need to be right and his desire to tell others how right he is are learned behaviors that can be *unlearned*. They can be changed. Becoming a controlling husband, and staying that way, is a *choice* and not a curse. It will take time, but change is both possible and attainable. A man can learn that he doesn't always have to be right.

Question 3: Can He Change?

Yes, he can change. If I can change, your husband can change. The question is not whether he *can* change, but *will* he change? This book will provide the understanding of the problem and tools necessary for change to occur. It will also help you understand what can motivate him to change and how you can be a positive influence in that process.

Patricia Evans addressed this question in detail in her 2006 book *The Verbally Abusive Man: Can He Change?*[3] Ms. Evans has spoken in many venues and written several books on the subject of verbal abuse and is often cited as one of the leading experts in this area. She clearly states in this book that change is possible for verbally abusive men, and she also presents suggestions for ways in which change can occur. I highly value the contribution she has made to the field by bringing the issue of verbal abuse to the forefront of our conversation, and no book on controlling husbands would be complete without addressing her work. However, it is worth noting a few differences between her books on verbal abuse and this book on controlling husbands.

First, verbal abuse is only one small way that husbands control their wives. In fact, many controlling husbands are not verbally abusive, as their control is more manipulative or nonverbal. Evans defines verbal abuse as any statement that defines the other person in a negative manner (i.e., "You are a horrible wife" or "You are feeling sorry for yourself"). Her books may be more relevant to those individuals who intentionally make verbally abusive statements with the intent of hurting their partners with their words.

Second, Evans describes the problem of verbal abuse as stemming from men having a concept of a "dream woman" (who she describes as the personification of an abuser's unconscious, unintegrated self) that they try to superimpose on their partners. In this book I present a different approach that describes a variety of forces that lead husbands to control their wives, rather than focusing on only one causal explanation.

Third, Evans sees the solution to verbal abuse as involving both parties signing a contract, which the woman prepares and subsequently enforces, to discontinue all verbally abusive behavior. She also suggests many activities for verbally abusive men to engage in, including therapy, self-nurturing, and journaling, which she believes will lead to change. If the verbal abuse continues, she offers guidelines for how women can leave the relationship.

In contrast, I present a more relational approach to change based on my belief that although the husband is solely responsible for his own choices to act in a controlling manner, the wife also participates in allowing this behavior to develop and be maintained. Lasting transformation requires both parties to be actively involved in change. This book provides numerous, specific interventions that couples can take to discontinue and prevent controlling behavior in their marriage.

You can have hope that change is possible. There is no question that a desire to change is a requirement for change. If your husband truly does not value you as a person, wants to treat you in a disrespectful and hurtful manner, or wants out of the marriage, there is no reason to expect he will change. Again, I don't believe you would be reading this book if you did not believe at least part of him wants to change. It is my sincere belief that he can change, and I truly hope that this book provides both of you with the tools to make this happen.

7

The Seven Strategies Husbands Use to Control Their Wives

A journey is like marriage. The certain way to be wrong is to think you control it.

John Steinbeck

Over the years, I have observed seven different strategies that husbands use to control their wives. When I present these ideas in seminars, husbands and wives wholeheartedly endorse them as accurate, responding with laughter, embarrassment, and frustration, while sharing stories of how they play out in their marriages. Your husband may demonstrate one or all of these strategies.

In this chapter I describe each strategy, followed by a fictional story of a couple who represent it. I have encountered many of these situations in my counseling practice, my teaching career, or my own marriage. Each section will conclude with what I call A Better Way—selfless behaviors for husbands combined with behaviors wives can use to encourage selflessness in their husbands.

Before presenting these strategies, it may be helpful to review some practical suggestions regarding how a wife can encourage a controlling husband to consider less selfish behavior. I've alluded to some of these ideas previously and I will speak more about them in the chapters on transformation. However, it is important for a wife to understand how she can begin to encourage her husband to change, realizing that she isn't helpless in creating change in her marriage. Throughout this chapter I will offer specific suggestions on how to deal with each strategy. However, there are three principles that apply to all of these strategies.

First, religious beliefs can be powerful motivators for change, so a wife can use whatever moral code her husband believes in to help him consider his decisions. For example, if he believes in a faith that tells him to put the needs of others before himself, but his actions show him to be a hypocrite, helping him understand this contradiction can be instrumental in his transformation.

Second, a wife can help her husband see how his behavior is pushing her away from him, when he wants to keep her close. Your husband does want to be with you, even if he feels he needs to control you to protect himself or you from harm. If he didn't feel this way, he would simply leave. A wife can help her husband see how treating her with love and trusting her to return that love will result in a lasting relationship.

Third, when a couple has children, they can be a strong motivation for change. For me, my children proved to be the most powerful incentive for me to become a better man. Your husband may be able to lie to himself and blame you for his behavior, but there is an innocence in children that can effectively cut through those lies. When you help your husband clearly see the effect his selfish behavior has on his children, he may be much more willing to work with you and change.

1. The Intimidator

The Intimidator controls his wife through the use of anger. He raises his voice while sometimes using threatening body language.

The Intimidator has a look that says, *You don't want to push me on this*, in both subtle and direct ways. He lets his wife know there will be consequences if she doesn't go along with him. Intimidators don't believe they will "win" an argument on principle. They assume they will need some type of implied threat to get their way.

Often the Intimidator overreacts to small annoyances, leading his wife to change her behavior and do whatever she can to prevent the volcanic eruption. Something as simple as disagreeing over what brand of soup to buy at the grocery store can lead to an explosion. The Intimidator uses his anger and volatile responses to control his wife, making her afraid of an outburst or a public scene.

Janeen never knew what would set Darnelle off on one of his tirades. It could be leaving dishes in the sink or forgetting to pick up something he wanted. Tonight she dreaded his return home. She tried to make sure the house looked okay but knew it would never meet his standard of cleanliness. She made sure the kids did the chores he asked them to do but still expected it would not be enough. *It's not fair! I shouldn't have to make them finish a job he gave them to do!*

After Darnelle had been home for a while, Janeen was beginning to think things would be okay. He hadn't mentioned the house or chores and was distracted with work he brought home. As she began to back out of the garage to go to her choir practice, she heard the sickening crunch of metal on metal. She knew instantly what had happened. He had parked his car on the far side of their driveway, behind her car in the garage. *I told him never to park behind my car!* She'd been in such a hurry that she didn't look behind her and backed right into his car. *He is going to freak out when he sees the cars.*

Predictably, when Darnelle came running out, his first response was to yell, "How could you?! I can't believe you wrecked both our cars! What's wrong with you?" He never considered that it was an accident, let alone that it was partly his fault for leaving his car parked behind hers. He was more interested in yelling at her and assessing the damage than asking if she was okay. All he cared about were the cars, the insurance hassle, and the money involved.

A Better Way

Darnelle should have *listened* to Janeen and asked if she was okay, instead of threatening and yelling. He let his immediate reaction of anger overcome him, preventing any opportunity to remember that he had actually caused the problem by parking behind her.

Janeen can help him change this behavior by stopping him immediately and not allowing him to yell at her. She can set an immediate boundary, refuse to be treated that way, and tell him to take a break and say nothing until he calms down. For this to happen, Janeen will have to overcome any feelings of low self-esteem that could lead her to feel she deserves to be yelled at and her fear that confronting him could make him even angrier.

2. The Manipulator

The Manipulator takes a different approach to control, playing a variety of games. He doesn't openly threaten his wife, but he convinces her that decisions he wants her to make are actually her own ideas. The Manipulator usually wants to lead his wife to choose what he wants without her ever knowing she has been manipulated.

He is not always this subtle though. Often he uses extensive overmanagement to direct and control aspects of his wife's life. He leaves lists of tasks for her to complete, leading her to wonder if she should make decisions without asking his opinion. In many cases, women who are married to a Manipulator have never had strong self-esteem, having been told in childhood or previous relationships that they were not capable of making good decisions.

"Have you thought about what would you like to do this weekend, honey?"

Sarah wondered why she was being asked, since John usually planned things, but she was glad he wanted her opinion. "I haven't really thought about it."

John mentioned that the mountains were nice this time of year.

Sarah, with her customary compliance, smiled and said, "That sounds nice." She really wanted to give it some thought, but John would get impatient with her if she didn't come up with an answer right away.

She was glad he wanted to spend time with her. She was thinking, *Dinner and a movie sound less stressful, but if I suggest that, he might change his mind and not want to do anything with me.*

Just then, John said, "I think you have a good idea. The mountains sound like fun."

She looked at him strangely and asked, "Weren't the mountains your idea?"

John turned slowly and said, "Well, it had crossed my mind, but I think you were the one who said that going up this weekend sounded like a nice idea. I just know it's pretty up there this time of year."

She was confused. *I don't remember that. I thought he brought up going to the mountains.*

He smiled and said, "The mountains are a great idea, sweetheart. Just don't ever say we don't do things that you want to do!"

A Better Way

John did not need to be manipulative. He could have simply been *honest* with Sarah, told her he wanted to go to the mountains, and asked her what she wanted to do.

Sarah could have encouraged this by refusing to play the manipulation game as soon as he asked her what she wanted to do. Saying she hadn't thought about it only transferred the choice back to him. If she had made her choice known, it would not have given the control back to John. Instead of just thinking, *I wish I had time to think about this*, she should have said it out loud, letting John know she needed time to think. Then later she could have offered her own suggestion about what she wanted to do.

John didn't have the ability to *make* her think or do anything—she simply gave up her power to him without a fight. Sarah will have to avoid the tendency to be quiet and let John have his way just to avoid conflict, as this only reinforces his tendency to control her.

3. The Sports Fan

Many of you know the Sports Fan. This is the husband who schedules the family's activities around the game. However, it is the outcome of the game that can really create problems. The entire home environment changes if his team loses. He becomes depressed or angry and is easily offended, taking his frustration out on the closest target. Sports become more than a hobby and turn into a way of life.

Maria dreaded the opening week of football season. She thanked God the Cowboys were playing an easy team on Sunday. Hector's demeanor changed during the game; he would yell and scream with a passion for his Dallas Cowboys that made absolutely no sense to her. *Doesn't he know that it is just a game?*

Maria never played sports and she didn't understand their importance to Hector. She felt like he valued football more than her. She watched him during the game and wondered how this could be fun. He looked so upset when the game didn't go well. On a day when his Cowboys lost to a much weaker team, he was distant, dismissive, and frustrated all night long, just as Maria knew he would be. She sighed, remembering how it often took Hector twenty-four hours or more to return to normal.

A Better Way

Hector and Maria would be better off using a skill I call *trading off*. Maria doesn't have to demand that Hector give up watching football but certainly she can refuse to be treated poorly during or after a game. If Hector can't control his emotions during a game, he could tape the game and watch it when Maria has other things to do. Or Maria could also arrange to go to a movie with a girlfriend on football afternoons, letting Hector know that by the time she returns home, he is no longer allowed to let any frustration about the game bleed over into their marriage.

Hector needs to respect Maria and do as she asks, choosing to value her over football. If Maria can offer a plan that gives Hector what he wants (football), even if he has to give something up in return (his negative attitude), then the marital relationship can become cooperative rather than competitive. Maria can be instrumental in making this type of change happen by suggesting a negotiated settlement rather than making each conflict a winner-take-all scenario.

4. The Pouter

The Pouter controls in a different way from the men we have met so far; he wants his wife to feel sorry for him and controls through becoming sullen, withdrawn, and sad. He uses guilt to get what he wants with the old "misery loves company" approach. When he is upset, the Pouter believes that everyone else in the family ought to be upset. In this way, he remains the center of attention, as the entire family walks on eggshells until he calms down or feels better.

Lisa knew before she ever opened her mouth that she would regret her words. Years of disappointment had convinced her of the futility of getting her hopes up. Despite this knowledge, she looked Andy in the eye and told him how she felt. "I really like this restaurant. Just because you are uncomfortable with all the kids at that table next to us, that's no reason to leave. I would like to stay."

It would have been easier to go along with what he wanted and just go eat somewhere else. In many ways, she would prefer him to get angry. *I know how to deal with a tantrum but how am I supposed to deal with childish pouting?* Andy's response was as passive as it was aggressive: he stared at his plate, refused to talk, and generally ruined the meal.

Every time one of the kids at the next table yelled or cried, Andy looked at them with frustration and muttered under his breath. Before the check even arrived, Lisa felt guilty and wondered, *I didn't do anything wrong. Why do I feel this way?* All of the drama exhausted her, and Lisa wished she had just gotten up and left when Andy said that's what he wanted.

A Better Way

Lisa's initial response was picture perfect. She told Andy the truth and *set clear boundaries*, giving him an opportunity to choose his response. Andy chose to pout and ruin the meal. This is when Lisa could have stood her ground and set another boundary. Rather than putting up with his childish pouting, she could have suggested they move to another table. If he continued to pout, she could call a taxi to take her home, although this could escalate the situation.

Andy will not continue to pout if pouting has no effect. When he learns that the most effective way of getting his needs met is to identify the problem and work with Lisa to come up with a solution, pouting will become unnecessary.

5. The Incompetent

The Incompetent husband has developed the unique skill of controlling by pretending to be helpless. He acts as though he can't do things that he doesn't want to do. I can already hear some of the wives saying: "You don't understand, Dr. Welch! He really can't cook! I wouldn't want to have to eat what he makes!"

Many husbands can cook quite well if they want to—men who can recite baseball statistics of their favorite players from 1978 can certainly follow a recipe. It's just easier to compliment their wives on how well they cook, tell them they wish they had the skill and talent their wives have in the kitchen, and avoid having to do all that work.

Should a wife begin to think her husband is capable of cooking, the husband simply reminds her about "The Great Pancake Incident of 2004," and she agrees that he should remain banished from the kitchen. By the way, the reason almost all husbands barbecue is because it's fun. Watch your husband when you have friends over for a barbecue. He shows off his new grill like it's a new car. He could learn to make crepes if motivated to do so, but burning meat on the grill is so much more fun.

Men certainly pretend to be incompetent in more areas than just cooking. Think about all the things you do because he says he "can't," when it may be more accurate to say he "won't." Planning parties, dusting the house, paying the bills . . . I don't know what your husband says he can't do. Just be aware that it is often easier to say he is unable to do something than to make the effort to learn how to do it.

Danielle was preparing for an afternoon appointment but she was running late. With car keys in hand, she noticed Marcus coming in from mowing the lawn.

"What's for lunch?" he asked.

She looked at him, wondering why feeding him was her responsibility and suggested tuna fish.

"But I can't make that. You always do it!"

"Are you really going to tell me you can't use a can opener?"

"You know I can't stand the smell of that mayonnaise," Marcus said.

Seriously! Do you think I like the smell of tuna fish? she thought. "It just doesn't taste the same when I make it, honey!"

Danielle looked at him rather dismissively, set the tuna can on the counter, and left for her appointment thinking, *Really? When will he grow up?*

A Better Way

Marcus could have prevented this entire conflict if he had simply chosen to try to do something new to make Danielle's life easier. He has to stop and consider how Danielle feels before he says anything. If he had thought about her needs, he would have realized that she had an appointment and made his own lunch.

Danielle definitely set a clear boundary there. In fact some readers may be thinking, *You go, girl! That was outstanding!* Marcus had to either fix his own lunch or be hungry, which is perfectly acceptable. Here's the problem—the end result, although better than giving in, was really more of an ultimatum than a cooperative solution.

If Danielle wanted to go a step beyond setting the boundary, she could tell Marcus directly that pretending to be unable to do things is the same as lying. She could ask for *honesty and equality* in their relationship. For instance, if Marcus really hates fixing tuna fish so much that he would be willing to clean all the toilets in the house in return for her fixing the sandwich, she might take that deal. Setting a boundary is a great start, but cooperation and negotiation is the higher goal.

6. The Mute

The Mute has mastered the use of the classic silent treatment. His lack of response gives him a great deal of power, especially if his wife wants or needs to feel a connection. The Mute can send the same message by paying attention to other things while she is speaking or looking right through her while she is talking. He may text or answer emails, watch the game on TV, or do anything but focus on her. This sends the loud and clear message that she is not as important as he is and what he is doing comes before her.

George was being quiet, and Robin knew something was wrong. *What happened last night?* She tried to recall everything they did. *We had dinner, and he helped Johnny with his homework. I was watching TV, and he sat down . . . Oh, that was it.*

She was watching a reality show that she liked but George hated. He wanted to watch a basketball game but he missed it because Robin watched her show.

Now she wondered what to do. *Should I leave him alone or ask what's wrong? What does he want me to do?*

Robin hated it when people were upset with her. She just wanted everyone to get along. Finally she said, "You know I hate it when you give me the silent treatment—why won't you just talk to me?" But George said nothing. Finally, Robin gave up and quit trying to make him talk. *I wish he would just get mad and yell. That would be better than this.*

A Better Way

This is a tough one. Robin can't make George talk, and his silence gives him power. It seems as if there is no way to win when your husband freezes you out, right? Continuing to guess what's wrong and trying to make him talk makes you feel helpless and childish. Robin can demand that George talk and make ultimatums, but he will probably just ignore her.

Of course, George has the ability to solve this situation quite easily. Remaining silent is an extremely selfish act, while telling Robin what is bothering him would open up the lines of communication. This is one of the best examples of passive-aggressive behavior, as George is acting in an extremely destructive manner by doing nothing. He needs to be more concerned with resolving the issue than remaining in control.

So what can Robin do? One option is to change the scenery. Sometimes changing the environment can give a husband a way to save face and change the game—maybe taking a walk or going to dinner will decrease the tension. Or Robin could say something like, "I'm sorry if I offended you, George, but there is no way to resolve this without talking. When you are ready to talk, let me know."

The main point here is that you can't make your husband talk and you also can't let his pity party prevent you from going about your daily activities. Robin did the right thing. She *refused to play the game* but she also needs to avoid blaming herself and hold George accountable for his behavior.

7. The Paranoid

The Paranoid controls his wife through fear born of anxiety, which can result in mistrust, suspicion, and jealousy. These men end up looking like micromanagers on steroids, as they are aware of every detail in their wives' daily activities. The Paranoid doesn't want his wife to go anywhere that might lead to risk or danger; he is sure something will go wrong.

The Paranoid may be excessively jealous. Sometimes he feels that if his wife has other friends, she must not truly love him or he must not be enough for her. He is afraid that his wife will leave him for someone else. The paranoia is grounded in extreme insecurity, which fuels the jealousy and turns into possessiveness, bitterness, and resentment. Though he may try to portray himself as capable and any woman's dream husband, he really sees himself as incompetent and unlovable.

When Kevin confronted Lucy as soon as she got home, she began to understand the extent of Kevin's jealousy. "You said you would be home at four and it's almost five," he said with an accusing glare.

"I got home as soon as I could. My workout just took longer tonight."

"I really don't like you going to the gym without me," Kevin said. "You know all those guys are looking at you."

"This is why I don't even like to go anymore," she responded. "You take all the fun out of it. I used to be so relaxed and happy and now I just worry about you getting mad if I talk to another man."

"You don't know how men think—these guys are just waiting for an opportunity with you."

"Kevin, you don't get it. I love you. Why can't you believe that?"

A Better Way

There is a point at which you cannot deal with this situation on your own. Severe jealousy, like anger, makes it mandatory to *seek professional help*. Jealous husbands have to learn to *face their fears*, and this may not be possible without group or individual counseling.

If Kevin and Lucy catch this process early enough, they might be able to talk about what's happening, but this rarely works. The insecurity and fear that drive his jealousy have likely been developing over many years and many relationships. The good news is that, with professional help, Kevin has a chance to face his fear and learn to trust his wife in ways he never dreamed possible.

Putting It All Together

When I talk to wives about the seven strategies, they invariably say, "I didn't have a name for it, but that is exactly what he does! Now I know what to call it." When I present these strategies to husbands, they feel somewhat ashamed, and that's okay. Guilt isn't a bad thing—it is what it is. Husbands need to learn from it.

Watch your relationship over the next few weeks. Identifying when these seven strategies occur is the first step to intervening and transforming this behavior. When you see it happening, stop and point it out. Make the choice to use one of the alternatives you have learned in this chapter. If you can learn to prevent even one of these strategies from happening, the effects on your relationship will be impossible to miss.

Part Three

Why You Allow Him to Control You

The Perfect Storm of Submission

8

Storm Front 1

Fear of His Anger

To decide to be at the level of choice is to take responsibility for your life and to be in control of your life.

Arbie M. Dale

In October of 1991, three seemingly unrelated events led to a storm of such immense magnitude, it became the focus of the 2000 movie *The Perfect Storm*. The movie told the story of the sinking of the fishing vessel *Andrea Gail* and the death of her crew. The power of Hurricane Grace collided with a storm system from the Great Lakes and a low-pressure system coming out of New England, resulting in one of the most devastating storm systems in history, with rogue waves reaching over one hundred feet high.

The experience that women who marry controlling husbands have is just such a perfect storm, with three storm fronts colliding to create potential disaster. Fear of her husband's anger boiling up from the south runs head-on into a pattern of learned helplessness driving down from the north. When these two fronts meet a low-pressure system of decision-making issues from the east, the result is a Perfect Storm of intense magnitude.

Why Am I Married to Him?

We've spent quite a bit of time talking about what makes controlling husbands tick. Let's shift gears for a bit and talk about wives. Just exactly why are you married to a man who controls you? Maybe you are holding on to the belief that he can be the man you thought he was. You see glimpses of that man, and there are many other qualities you love about him. You don't want to give up on him. Besides, he isn't like that *all* the time.

Perhaps there are some pieces from your past involved here—how you were treated as a child, self-esteem issues, things you thought you had locked away that are rearing their ugly heads again. Maybe your father was rather dominant and being with your partner feels oddly comfortable, even though there are aspects of the experience you don't like. There may be some truth to the idea that you have grown accustomed to letting him do things for you. It's not all bad when someone takes care of you and makes sure you are protected. In fact his ability to handle things may be one of the reasons you fell in love with him. Still, you probably hear that small voice at times scolding you for not speaking up.

All of these issues can come together to convince a woman to remain in a relationship with a power differential. Some say women who stay in these relationships are weak, are not very intelligent, or like being controlled. I don't think the issue is nearly that simple.

I am fully aware that Jan had many reasons to leave me. Here's the thing: her decision to stay with me and try to help me become a better man has led to a really wonderful transformation in our marriage. If she had given up on me, we never would have had that opportunity. Remaining in a controlling relationship and simply accepting the behavior is self-destructive, but identifying the behavior, expecting change from your partner, and holding him accountable for change will transform your marriage.

One of the primary reasons women allow men to control them is fear. For some women, this happens when their husband talks over them when they are speaking. For others, it's when their husband raises his voice with a threatening tone and gives them a look that says, "Don't push me." He may stand in the doorway and not let you leave the room. He could even use the dreaded "D" word and threaten to leave the marriage and sue for custody of the children.

In most cases, the couple is quite skilled at keeping these interactions secret. They are too embarrassed to tell their friends or family, and he wants to maintain the stable family image. If one partner makes a mistake and a small window to the truth is opened, both quickly provide a plethora of explanations like, "Oh, he was just tired," or, "It wasn't what it looked like."

The Effects of Anger

From an early age, my wife, Jan, had to deal with a father who had pretty significant anger problems. She believes that her father never really recovered from the loss of his first child to a brain tumor. Perhaps it was easier to be angry than to deal with his own pain. In any case, her father's anger took its toll on her. Whenever it was time for him to come home, she would quickly inspect the house to be sure she had not forgotten to put everything in its place.

She believed that if she could just be careful enough, she could avoid the hours of lecturing and yelling that would result if she had done something wrong. Despite her best attempts, she would usually fail in thinking of everything she was supposed to have done, and more often than not, he would explode in anger, destroying her self-esteem. She came to consider herself a failure and eventually as unlovable. Her relationship with her father left her believing that she deserved to be treated with disrespect and disdain.

Consider your own responses to threatening or intimidating situations. Think of the interactions you had with the "mean girl" at school or the tyrannical boss in one of your first jobs. When you didn't respond by giving in to their demands, they upped the ante, using threatening words or actions until you gave in. The next time, the bully didn't even have to make the threat, knowing you would give in just based on the perceived threat. The bully may even have been your father.

In many marriages this feeling of fear, insecurity, and imprisonment occurs in response to the husband's anger. In reality, it boils down to the wife being bullied by her husband. When I talk over my wife or raise my voice, I am being a bully. The effect of this experience and the increasing damage to a woman and her self-esteem create a dilemma. On the one hand, she fears the threatening clouds and can see the storm is growing stronger. *I know I'm scared, but this is a relationship I committed to for a lifetime. I said that I was in it for better or worse, right? Well, this is the worst, or at least the worst so far.* On the other hand, she just doesn't know how much more she can take.

The Calm *after* the Storm

In relationships like these, the time before the storm is filled with anxiety and activity. Rather than a calm before the storm, there is a calm *after* the storm. This phenomenon may sound familiar to some of you reading this book. Sometimes, you are glad the danger has passed and you want to enjoy the calm after the storm. Other times, you want to confront him. You want to say, "No! You don't get to say I'm sorry and think it's all better! You promised not to act that way again, and I started to believe you might actually mean it. That's not fair!" You are smart enough to know that if you push it, you might just head right back into the storm. Your fear is too strong, so you remain silent. You know that he is scrambling to find a way back into your good graces, and it's what you want too. Just like Camelot, for that one, brief, shining moment, you feel loved, accepted, and happy.

The peace and quiet after the storm are very appealing. This is an environment in which a wife is tempted to downplay her husband's recent behavior.

Denise was always making excuses for Ken's explosions of anger. "He had a hard day at work. The kids were really out of control. I shouldn't have pushed him so hard." *If I just let him have his way, he won't get mad, and then we can have a quiet evening.* She soon realized that the faster she gave in to his will and demands, the less she had to deal with his anger. To make sure this happened, she had to excuse his behavior. She would tell herself, *He has so many good qualities. This isn't really that big a deal.* She believed that if she could do a better job picking up around the house, he wouldn't get so angry.

You may do the same thing in your relationship. Men like this are often highly intelligent and capable, and your husband probably does many things to make you feel loved, especially when he feels guilty. You tell yourself that he really does love you, and that he doesn't really mean what he says when he's angry. Sometimes, you actually believe it.

Over time, it becomes a dance that you both learn well. He feels insecure and anxious, so he tries to make those feelings go away by controlling you. You get hurt in the process, but your tendency to blame yourself for his problems leads you to make excuses for him. You know he will apologize and treat you like a princess afterward, so you learn to simply wait for the good stuff and put up with the bad. This is just what marriage is to you.

Dot, Daddy?

Sometimes, the anger can ruin an experience that would otherwise be very positive. This is what happened when we were moving from

Memphis, Tennessee, to Denver back in 2001. I try to organize things to relieve my anxiety and I had created a wonderful color-coded system for organizing all our boxes. I had purchased some colored dots and stuck them on every box so we would know where they went in our new house in Denver.

Our three-year-old son, Brevin, had been having some fun of his own. Brev had been following me around after I marked each set of boxes. He had painstakingly taken dots off some boxes and put them on other boxes. He also kept many for himself, as he was covered in dots from head to toe. While I was in another room, Jan noticed what Brevin was doing and began laughing hysterically. I came out to see what all the commotion was about, and my son looked up at me with stickers on every finger and calmly said, "Dot, Daddy?"

Looking back, this should have been one of the most hilarious and wonderful memories of our parenting years. My wife still laughs whenever we mention it, for she truly enjoyed the experience. I, on the other hand, responded with anger and frustration rather than laughter. In my defense, our son had ruined hours and hours of work, but the expression on his face was truly priceless. He thought he had been extremely helpful!

The world looks much different to me when I allow myself to sit back, look at what's happening, and find the proverbial silver lining in the situation. Sure, I had a few more hours of work to undo all the creative labeling my son had engaged in. But when these potentially anger-provoking situations occur now, I try to think about how to make the situation better for my family, rather than worse. Life is just too short to let anger and frustration ruin my life and that of my family.

Hope You Can Believe In

A wife can set boundaries that will affect her husband's behavior. If he threatens violence, you can involve others, including the police if necessary, to respond appropriately to dangerous threats or behavior. If he yells, you can set a standard that in this marriage, you will not yell at each other. That means you can't yell at him either. The new normal becomes speaking respectfully or not speaking at all. You can enforce this boundary by simply ending the conversation and not engaging with him if he breaks this rule.

If you can see his anger as a coping mechanism for the insecurity and fear he feels, you can talk to him about the real issues that are underneath his anger. Don't keep dancing the same dance; change the music. Help him learn to deal with his insecurity and fear without intimidation and anger.

Help him find a counselor to talk to if he is having trouble learning to control his temper. Go to appointments with him if he and his counselor feel it will help. Rather than assuming he is incapable of handling his anger, believe that he is capable of change. Help him work with anger-management groups or a counselor to learn how to control his emotions. The road to hope begins with your believing he is capable of controlling his anger and helping him get connected to the professionals who can teach him how to do it.

9

Storm Front 2

Learned Helplessness

While the storm system born out of fear of anger is developing in the south, in the north, another weather pattern is taking shape. Born out of years of wanting to please others to avoid their anger and disappointment, a pattern of compliance and self-depreciation is emerging. This system is about to run head-on into the storm system from the south.

When my wife shared the following story with me, I knew I had to share it with you. It provides an inside look at how a concept psychologists call *learned helplessness* develops.

Raggedy Andy

This is what Jan told me.

"One of the most vivid memories I have is of an early birthday when I was turning five or six years old. I woke up to a huge box wrapped in bright orange paper. My birthday was three days after Christmas, so my parents usually just gave me a combination gift. I always felt my birthday didn't really matter much.

"This year was different. This enormous box was all mine and it was special just for my birthday! I ripped off the orange wrapping and found a brand-new Raggedy Andy doll! He was bigger than I was. I couldn't wait to introduce him to the Raggedy Andy doll I already had—the one I loved to dance all around my room with. I just knew they would be the best of friends! I ran down the hall to my room, hurried inside, and then stopped short in my tracks.

"My Andy, the one I loved so much, was not lying on the bed where I had left him. I looked all over my room, under the bed, behind the bed. I left the brand-new Raggedy Andy lying in a heap on the floor, as my only concern was finding my treasured friend. I could not find him anywhere, and my mother saw how upset I was. She took me aside and whispered that since I had a new, bigger, and better Andy, I wouldn't need the old one anymore. She told me that they were giving my Andy away to another little girl since I had a new one.

"I was heartbroken. A toy doesn't matter as much as the relationship you develop with it over the years. I didn't want a new, bigger Andy. I wanted the one with the treasured friendship that years of wear and tear and love had created.

"I remember pleading with my mother to give the other little girl the new Raggedy Andy and let me have my old, well-loved Andy back. She refused, telling me that it was already gone and there was nothing she could do about it.

"I felt as if my heart had been ripped out and no one cared enough to listen to my empty pleas. There was no consoling me or my broken heart. The huge new Raggedy Andy I had been given was left untouched and unloved in a corner. How could I love that new Andy? Who knew when he would be replaced and taken away just like my old friend? I wasn't going to be burned twice so I didn't go near him.

"I still believed that my friend Andy was somewhere in the house. I just wanted to say good-bye and hold him one more time, to see his bright face and the love hidden underneath the beautiful heart painted on his chest. A few days later, I decided to look in my father's office, even though we were forbidden to go in there. Sure enough, I found my beloved Andy hidden there. Andy's big smile lit up the room, and my heart jumped for joy when I ran to him and hugged him tightly. I remember so vividly how safe I felt in his arms once again.

"That feeling was to last only a few minutes though. My mother discovered me in my father's office and tried to take my beloved Andy from me. The tears streamed down my face, and for just a moment, I thought my mother would relent. However, she told me they had already agreed to give the doll away. Despite my request, she told me that my father would not even consider giving the new doll away instead. She did let me have one last dance with my dear friend.

"My face stained with tears, I held the friend that I knew I would never see again. The Raggedy Andy that I had loved so well had elastic straps on his feet so you could dance with him and a music box inside that played beautiful music. I slowly wound the knob on the back as I sat holding him, and when the music started, I stood up and slowly started to spin and dance around the room. I was desperately trying to find a way to say good-bye to my loyal friend, not understanding why he had to be taken away from me. I said good-bye in the only way I knew—by holding him as tightly as I possibly could.

"When the music ended, I slipped his feet off of mine, held him close to my heart one last time, kissed his check, and handed him to my mom. To this day, I still remember the depth of the sorrow I felt. I think that was the beginning of my lifelong belief that the world was not a safe place and that you had to put up as many walls as possible to protect yourself.

"I did come to love my new Raggedy Andy in new and different ways. He became the one I ran to when tears streamed down my face from so many more disappointments I would face as a child. To this day, the new Andy that I grew to love sits on a bed in our home. He had been worn with age, but as an anniversary gift one year, Ron took him to a professional doll repair shop to return him to beautiful condition.

"Perhaps the loss of my childhood friend prepared me to deal with my sister's death, my mother's death, and the years of pain and sadness created by my father's anger. I only know that the intentional ripping away of my childhood friend by parents who were supposed to love me taught me that I couldn't trust anyone with anything that mattered to me. The innocence of my childhood was lost in that one devastating experience, but the effects of that experience are with me to this day."

Love, Loss, and Abandonment

The experience of having her childhood friend taken away from her set the stage for a series of losses that created a "learned helplessness" process for Jan. She began to believe that no matter what she did, she could not hold on to those she loved. This was translated into a general negative expectation that it wasn't really worth even trying to prevent bad things from happening.

Losing the ones you love can be overwhelming. Some people shy away from ever loving again, building walls that prevent anyone from getting close to them. Others choose to believe that loneliness is simply their lot in life, remaining depressed and even suicidal, giving up any expectation of happiness or fulfillment. Still others put their hope in the future, waiting for the day when their dreams come true. One of the reasons that Jan allowed me to treat her the way she did in our early years was that so many people she loved had abandoned her. Her sister died before she knew her, her mother was lost in a world of mental illness, while the grief and resentment her father felt led him to treat her in angry, destructive ways.

Jan believes that the losses she experienced were central in the formation of the person she became as an adult. She felt it was her responsibility to make everyone happy. She sacrificed her own happiness many times just to be sure others would smile or feel good. After the death of her sister, Jan's mom became very depressed for many years. Her mom clung to Jan, and Jan felt an obligation to provide her company, listen to her problems, and make her happy.

Jan experienced several more losses. Her mother was unable to take care of Jan and her sisters due to her depression, forcing her mother and two of the girls to move in with her grandmother. Eventually Jan went to live with her father, and she and her older sister stayed with her father for the remainder of her childhood years. Her mother and grandmother told her that her decision to live with her father caused her mother's depression; they blamed her for rejecting her mother. Tragically, her mother continued to struggle with depression, and she died just after Jan turned eighteen.

Learned Helplessness and Dependence

Psychologist Aaron Beck points out that individuals with dependent personality styles view themselves as "inherently inadequate and helpless" in a dangerous situation, while also believing that the solution is to find someone who can solve their problems and take care of them.[1] Unfortunately, this is often a case of the cure being worse than the problem. For some women, a previous jealous boyfriend or a dominant and abusive father may have set the tone for future relationships. They have learned that discretion is the better part of valor, staying out of the battle rather than risking more harm.

This way of dealing with life's challenges is known as *learned helplessness*.[2] Martin Seligman coined this term while working with experimental dogs. Some of these dogs could escape from the electrical shocks they were given, while others could not. Initially, the dogs who could not avoid being shocked still tried to avoid the pain, but eventually they gave up and quit trying. Later, when they were placed in a situation where they could escape the shocks, they didn't try to get away, as they had learned they were helpless.

A wife can adopt learned helplessness when she doesn't like something in the relationship but quickly learns that trying to change it doesn't work. Soon she stops trying to make changes and accepts the way things are. She learns that no effort on her part will allow her to escape it, so she just quits trying to escape. As this process is repeated, the wife's self-esteem slowly erodes.

One couple I worked with, whom I will call Wendy and Bob, displayed this phenomenon. After church they were talking about what Pastor John had said about headship and submission in marriage. The pastor had talked about a Christian model of marriage in which the husband is the leader of the home and the husband is called to sacrifice everything, including his life, for his wife.

Wendy thought about bringing up this issue with Bob. *I don't really understand the whole submission thing. What if something is more important to me than it is to him? I don't think I can count on him to choose what I want over what he wants, so how do I ever get my needs met?*

Each time Wendy considered saying something to Bob, she thought of how easy it was for him to talk her out of her opinion. She remembered the many times she had voiced her opinion and he had done what he wanted anyway. By the time they pulled into the driveway, she had decided that it wasn't worth the effort and she should just accept what the pastor said and assume wives were just less important in a marriage.

However, in the counseling session that occurred soon after this, Wendy decided it was safe enough to confront Bob by relating the entire internal conversation she had experienced after church. As she described the thoughts and feelings she had gone through, he looked at her rather incredulously. When she was done, he said, "I just thought you were really quiet on the way home and had nothing to say."

Bob was genuinely surprised that she had become so used to his not listening to her that she had decided not to even try to tell him what she was thinking. For one of the first times in therapy, he didn't respond with an argument but just sat there in silence. Eventually he said, "I didn't know. I can't believe you are so scared to talk to me."

This turned out to be a huge turning point in our work together. These types of difficult interactions provide amazing opportunities for transformation.

I asked Bob whether his primary concern was that his wife agree with him so that he won the argument or that she feel honored and respected for her own views. He had to admit that, based on his actions, he was more concerned about convincing her to believe what he believed than he was about listening to her views and understanding them.

This pattern in their relationship had become so repetitive that Wendy admitted she rarely even tried to have an opinion. She said, "It's easier to just agree with whatever he says. There's less hassle that way." This is a perfect example of learned helplessness.

Through a great deal of hard work in counseling, they were able to change this core belief system. Wendy had to risk sharing her feelings and the rejection that might cause. Bob was devastated to realize that his wife didn't feel that he loved and valued her.

He began to realize how much he had controlled her and decided that this was not how he wanted her to feel or how he wanted to live his life. He said he understood she avoided telling him how she felt out of fear of his response. Wendy began to have a voice in the marriage when they decided to change how they communicated. They agreed that Wendy would always share her thoughts and feelings with Bob. In turn, Bob agreed not to try to talk her out of her feelings but to restate what she said and respect her views. This change proved to be the catalyst for many more positive changes in their marriage.

The Learned Helplessness Marriage Quiz

Take this short quiz to see if you are experiencing learned helplessness in your relationship.

1. Do you do what your husband tells you to do out of fear of his retribution?
2. Do you avoid things you wish you had the freedom to do because of how he will react?
3. Do you ask him first about any activity you might start in case he doesn't want you to do it?
4. Do you have a mental list of people you can't see, places you can't go, and things you can't do because he wouldn't like it?
5. When you consider doing something, is your first thought, *What would he think?*
6. If you ever think about leaving the relationship, are you scared that he would react in ways that could be harmful to you or your children?

There is no fancy statistical formula to score this quiz, as it is simply a screening questionnaire. However, if you answered any of these items affirmatively, you may be experiencing some learned helplessness. If you answered three or more affirmatively, I believe you should consider that learned helplessness may be a core pattern in your marriage.

Learned Helplessness and Self-Esteem

I coach youth sports. I have worked with young men for many years coaching baseball, basketball, and soccer while both my sons were growing up. I have always thought that failure was more a state of mind than an actual experience.

Often players see a missed shot or a strikeout as a failure. I coached one especially distraught young man who was visibly defeated as he walked back to the dugout after striking out to end a game with the bases loaded. I sat down by him and asked him how he judged success and failure. He answered, through his tears, "It's kinda obvious, Coach. I didn't hit the ball. I failed."

I asked him if he had used the hitting mechanics he had been taught, and he said that he had. I asked him if he had swung with his best effort and chosen good pitches to swing at. He again said that he had. I looked at him and told him that in my mind, based on what he had said, I thought he had succeeded. He looked up at me with confusion and said, "You're crazy, Coach. I struck out and we lost. That's not success."

As we talked, I realized that he was using the wrong measuring stick. You see, baseball is a game of failure. My coaches taught me that over and over again when I played. The best hitters in the Major Leagues *fail* seven out of ten times they go up to the plate. You are *supposed* to fail most of the time. The key is to enjoy the successes. This young man had been taught to judge success and failure by the result of his actions, rather than the actions themselves. A few minutes talking with a coach doesn't change a lifetime of negative thoughts and perceptions. It will take a long time, and a lot of positive affirmations, for this young man to truly change his thinking and give himself credit for the successes he has in life.

You can learn from this young baseball player. His story illustrates how you can overcome learned helplessness. Life is full of disappointments and frustrations, but there are a lot of high points on the journey as well. If you give up because you have failed a few times, you lose the opportunity for success. More importantly, this analogy is relevant because in sports, as in life, situations (and people) can change.

Consider your answers to the previous quiz. If your responses showed that you avoid things you want to do or are hesitant to do things because you lack confidence, these are opportunities for overcoming the symptoms of learned helplessness. Your answers may say that you don't go places or do things because of your relationship with your husband, but you can learn to become more assertive and positive in your responses.

I suggest you take three steps to begin to overcome learned helplessness. First, try to make changes in small decisions that have less significant consequences. If you are able to succeed in small ways, you can move on to larger choices. Second, you need to talk about your desire to have a stronger voice with your husband. He needs to know that you often make decisions out of fear of his response, and although you may not believe it, he may actually want to help you change this. Last, consider having a friend serve as an accountability partner with you to encourage you and motivate you to change this part of your personality. It will take time, but the effects on your self-esteem and happiness will be profound.

10

Storm Front 3

Decision Making and Submission

It does not take much strength to do things, but it requires great strength to decide on what to do.

Elbert Hubbard

As the first two storm fronts continue to grow, the prevailing winds in the east long ago developed a third weather pattern of immense power. Some of our strongest behavior patterns, including how we make decisions, begin in early childhood. One person may learn to remain quiet to survive in the chaos of family life, while another learns to stand up and fight for what he or she wants. These patterns develop further in adolescent and early adulthood relationships.

For couples who follow a Christian system of belief, words like *submission* and *headship* are often heard, describing a perceived difference in power in the marital relationship. The belief that there is a difference in power between husbands and wives is integrated into the way decisions are made in the marriages of many Christian couples. However, many other Christian and non-Christian couples prefer to view both partners as having equal power in the decision-making process in marriage.

In this chapter, we will explore models of decision making that couples use in marriage, as well as concepts such as headship and submission that are often involved in the process. The goal of the chapter is to provide you with the skills to make respectful, honorable decisions in your marriage.

Leadership or Control?

Many years ago I received a call from a prospective client who told me she was interested in counseling because she wanted to learn to be more submissive. I asked, "Can you tell me what you mean by submission, as people have many different understandings of that word?" She responded in a rather timid and sad voice, saying, "I guess I just need to honor my husband more. My pastor says I haven't been letting him lead me spiritually and I need to know how to do that."

You know how you hear someone say something and you just know there is more to the story? I knew that she might very well be right, and there might be ways in which she could learn to accept spiritual leadership from her husband. You know what my gut told me, though? She was married to a controlling husband.

Sure enough, when I met the couple for the first time and they shared their story, the issue had more to do with intimidation than spiritual leadership. The husband enforced authority in the home with power and control, using Scripture to validate his views. He was insecure in his role as a husband, thought of his own needs first, and dealt with his insecurity through convincing her to do what he wanted. He wasn't an evil man and he didn't enjoy hurting his wife's feelings or lowering her self-esteem. He just didn't know any other way.

Decision Making in a Marriage

You find out where the power is in your marriage when decisions have to be made. If you both generally agree on an issue, you can't really see who has the final say. Some couples claim to have a truly equal marriage, and while that is a great goal to strive for, it rarely happens. Most couples have a more dominant partner, or at least one who tends to argue better, is more comfortable with conflict, brings in more money, or is more powerful for one reason or another.

The decision-making power in your marriage can be seen in small or large conflicts. Suppose you have a vacation coming up and you have to decide where to go. Not a major decision but it is clearly a zero sum game; only one vacation spot can be chosen, at least for this trip. Both of you suggest different places. Where do you end up going? In other words, who has the power?

Maybe you have a much more important decision to make. Say you both have opportunities to move up in your careers. The problem is that your job advancement is in Boston and his is in L.A. Now what? This time the decision will have lifelong implications. How do you choose who gets the opportunity? There's no fair way to resolve this; someone wins and someone loses.

I see you, you in the back row with your mouth open. *You don't know how hard it is for me. I'd give anything to be in charge but I've given up trying. It's easier to not even try.* Since you brought it up, let me ask you this: When you don't get what you want, what do you do? I would bet that you have discovered many different ways to gain some power and control in less direct ways. I think you take control in ways you don't even realize.

You may choose to *decide not to decide*, resent your lack of input, and then get back at him by controlling other areas of your marriage. To quote Dr. Phil, "How's that workin' for you?" This is really just another form of learned helplessness, as you are giving up the opportunity to take control in a situation, settling for whatever decision he makes, and then getting back at him in other ways. Of course, there's a better way to make decisions that will draw you together rather than pulling you apart.

Before moving to three specific ways to transform decision making in your marriage, I want to discuss the Christian concepts of submission and headship. Unfortunately, these concepts have been used by Christian husbands to justify unhealthy marital behavior, but understanding their true meaning can shed a great deal of light on power and control in marriage.

Understanding the Concepts of Submission and Headship

The concept of submission gets a lot of bad press, but in fairness, that negative connotation is not entirely undeserved. We have applied modern concepts to a word that was not originally used as we now define it. Headship is often just as misunderstood.

The concepts of headship and submission appear several times in the New Testament (for example, 1 Cor. 11:3; Phil. 2:4; Col. 3:18–19). Paul's famous words in Ephesians 5, however, are the most often quoted: "Wives, submit yourselves to your own husbands as you do to the Lord. For the husband is the head of the wife as Christ is the head of the church, his body, of which he is the Savior. Now as the church submits to Christ, so also wives should submit to their husbands in everything. Husbands, love your wives, just as Christ loved the church and gave himself up for her" (Eph. 5:22–25).

I worked with a husband who brought in his Bible app in which he had highlighted the Ephesians passage about submission. He wasn't interested in reading on to the part where husbands are called to give up their lives for their wives. This narrow view, in which submission is solely defined in terms of power and control, does not hold up under scrutiny.

No discussion of submission is complete without talking about headship. They really are two ends of the same spectrum. When one partner is submitting, the other is often leading, and this can be a healthy process. However, headship often ends up looking more like control and domination than healthy leadership.

Internationally respected New Testament scholar Craig Blomberg,[1] a colleague of mine at Denver Seminary, tells me that he is not aware of any place in the Bible where the term *submit* does not mean to place under authority. However, the authority figure is told to be sacrificial and selfless in acting in the best interest of the person over whom he has authority. This would mean that even if the husband wanted to be selfish and choose his path, he is expected to think of his wife first and choose the path that will empower her. This is exactly the conclusion that I have reached after my own abuse of power in my marriage and years of counseling couples with power and control issues.

The authors of *Marriage at the Crossroads*, William and Aida Spencer and Steve and Celestia Tracy, offer differing viewpoints on equality in marriage. Nonetheless, they all agree that any type of headship resulting in power and control born out of fear of retribution is not biblical and is not what Paul intended in his letters to the Ephesians and the Corinthians. The Tracys point out that many influential evangelical writers encourage this type of inappropriate submission, giving the following example: Some teach that "the husband's headship means a wife must never try to change her husband and should passively accept his sin, must obey him even if it violates her conscience and sense of God's leading, is to follow his mission and dreams (not her own), [and] should be quiet or just say 'sure' when she disagrees with him."[2]

This model of headship ignores any concept of empowerment, building up the other partner, or strengthening the relationship. It is based on an expectation of the "head" being someone who mandates the behavior of the one who is serving him or her. This sounds more like a dictatorship than healthy leadership of a family. In a relationship based on love and respect, a husband might make a decision but would choose the option that best met the needs of his wife. In a truly healthy marriage, the husband has his wife's back, and she has his.

Boundaries and Submission

Henry Cloud and John Townsend, in their book *Boundaries*, present a theory of submission in which they highlight the importance of wives' setting appropriate boundaries. When a wife of a controlling husband begins to assert clear and healthy limits, these authors suggest that the husband can begin to change, as his wife is no longer "enabling his immature behavior." Although wives can't force their husbands to change, creating standards can help husbands see the consequences of their behavior.[3]

Boundaries are good, and in general, I'm a fan. However, learning to set these boundaries can be easier said than done. Let me illustrate a positive way to set boundaries with the story of Karen and Dwight.

Karen had heard enough. "You can't go play softball again tonight. We were going out to dinner—I got a babysitter and everything!"

Dwight retorted, "It's not my fault they rescheduled the game."

"But you promised, Dwight!"

"You want me to miss the game? Really?"

Karen thought about how to respond. *If I push this, he'll go to dinner but he'll ruin it. He won't be any fun to be with.*

Karen decided to set a boundary, as she had learned to do, but let Dwight know she understood the conflict he was facing.

"Dwight, I understand they changed the game, and that's not your fault. I know this is a tough choice for you. I'm just really disappointed and I want to ask you a question. I know that your team had more than enough players last game. Do you think you could call the guy who coaches the team and see if they would have enough without you?"

Dwight looked visibly calmer. "I'm glad you understand this isn't easy for me. I made a commitment to the team, but you're right, we had plenty for the last game. I know you have been looking forward to our date night—so have I. I guess it couldn't hurt to call and see if they have enough."

"Thanks, hon. That's all I'm asking. If you find out they would forfeit without you, I'll understand."

Dwight called the coach and discovered the team did have enough players without him. He told the coach he'd skip this game, and when he saw Karen's eyes light up as he told her they could go out, he realized he had made the right choice. *I'm just glad she saw my side of the story too*, he thought. They both really enjoyed their night out, and both were reminded how important it is to consider the other's point of view before overreacting in anger or frustration.

Submission is sometimes seen as a wife's codependent enabling. It can occur because the wife has seen the consequences of attempting to set boundaries, including the potential threat to herself and her children, and she chooses to give in to her husband's will rather than take the risk. I think it takes more than boundaries for a husband to begin to change, but it's a good place to start. Starting in chapter 13, I will present a model of transformation that leads to real change. This will not just involve your husband—it will include you changing also. Both of you have contributed to the control problems in your marriage, and it will take both to fix these problems.

In *Boundaries*, Cloud and Townsend remind us that the submission road runs both ways. They argue that controlling relationships occur when a husband tries to keep his wife as a slave "under the law." In their words, "We have never seen a 'submission' problem that did not have a controlling husband at its root."[4]

When the Church Is the Problem

Churches across America and the world endorse very different views on biblical models of marriage. These range from a complementarian view that says husbands and wives make different but complementary contributions to the relationship, to the egalitarian view that husbands and wives make more equal contributions. However, I have had numerous clients who have heard pastors preach that wives are called to simply agree with whatever husbands say at all times—a view that is not consistent with either biblical teaching or common sense.

Wives whose husbands have adopted this latter view can become depressed and then feel guilty about feeling depressed! This is reinforced when their female Christian friends tell them they would understand how to submit if they read the Bible and prayed more. Just what they need, friends adding more guilt by telling them they are not only failing as wives but failing as Christians too.

When a church endorses this type of dictatorial control in marriage, defining it as biblically supported headship and submission, that church becomes complicit in the destruction of these marriages and the people in them. There is simply no biblical evidence to support the view that wives need to accept second-class citizenship in marriage to please God.

Craig Blomberg noted the following in a 2011 blog post: "My main point is that no matter where you come down on the vexed term *kephalē*, usually translated 'head' in verse 23, *such headship is never a matter of privilege but only of responsibility*. . . . None of us as husbands will ever come close. But we know our marching orders. And in most cases it means replacing 'controlling' behavior with 'empowering' behavior."[5]

In my opinion, it is only in a climate of mutual respect, honor, selflessness, and dedication that biblical submission can take place without the development of a controlling, oppressive environment. In entirely too many couples, one partner submits to the other out of fear. The result is a stifling relationship in which a wife feels unloved, disrespected, dishonored, and controlled. In contrast, a relationship of mutual submission often results in mutual respect, honor, and love.

Three Transformational Decision-Making Skills

In my practice, as well as in other areas of my life, I have discovered three successful strategies that couples can use when they can't agree on a decision. Each of these strategies has its own benefits and challenges, but they are all consistent with an empowering, positive view of decision making and marriage. I call them the Three Transformational Decision-Making Skills.

Skill 1: After You . . . No, After You . . .

The first skill allows couples to utilize a simple process in which they make the final decision based on who will be most affected by the decision. In most decisions, there is one party who cares more about the outcome than the other. The couple may have differing perceptions of who this is but they can focus their energy on deciding who will be more directly affected or who has more invested in the decision.

Of course, one partner may end up with more decisions being made in their favor, but if the couple's goal is to build each other up, that shouldn't matter. It becomes an issue only if one partner is focused on getting their way at the expense of the other, as is the case with controlling husbands who refuse to change. We will discuss many different strategies for addressing power and control issues in later chapters.

Skill 2: Switch 'Em Up

I love this second skill. In this approach, both partners agree to stop advocating for their own desires and choose to argue for their spouse's hoped-for outcome. This can be fun for the couple if they approach it with an open mind. Again, it is consistent with a selfless model of marriage, as both partners encourage each other, thinking of the other's needs before their own.

I have had some of the most enjoyable sessions with couples using this approach to decision making. It is amazing how creative partners can become when they truly commit to helping their partner get what they want. In addition, the negative energy of selfishness is replaced with the positive strength of advocating for the partner's wishes. I have had couples tell me that when the process is over, they don't even remember why they ever fought for their own way!

Skill 3: Door #3

The third decision-making skill comes from the iconic game show *Let's Make a Deal*, in that the couple needs to choose a third option, one they come to through compromise. It involves agreeing to throw out the options currently on the table and come up with a compromise that will hopefully satisfy both parties. Compromise always involves giving something up, so both spouses have to accept that they will not get everything they want. This technique involves choosing to give the relationship priority over individual needs.

Compromise involves giving up some of what you want most in the situation and working to come up with an alternative that allows each party to get some of what they want. This is consistent with a selfless model of marriage, as each partner is thinking of the other's needs and trying to come up with a Door #3 alternative. Couples are often surprised to learn that the compromise they come up with is better than either Door #1 or Door #2.

My editor shared an example with me from her marriage. She and her husband had difficulty agreeing where to go out for dinner, so they made cards with dinner options like "husband picks place," "wife picks place," "husband picks place wife will like," "wife picks place under $12," or "husband picks new place." When they went out to dinner, they pulled a card out of the envelope and the decision was made!

These three skills can help you overcome the challenges of making decisions in a controlling relationship. Both parties have to agree to participate in the exercises, but the more you practice them, the more natural the skills will become. You may eventually find you can't even remember how you used to make decisions as your relationship becomes more empowering and positive right before your eyes.

Part Four

Niagara Falls and the Can Opener

Changing Your Marriage Right Now

11

Going over Niagara Falls

Admitting You Have a Problem

A man must be big enough to admit his mistakes, smart enough to profit from them, and strong enough to correct them.

John C. Maxwell

People who struggle with addictions say that admitting you have a problem is half the battle. You have probably already decided that there is, or at least might be, a problem with control in your marriage. Your partner may not agree, but you know that you can't stay on the same path you are on. The now famous definition of insanity, which has been attributed to both Albert Einstein and Ben Franklin, applies here: "Insanity is doing the same thing over and over again and expecting different results." Something has to change.

Husbands and wives seem to have great difficulty seeing their part in conflicts. It is so much easier to blame the other person. Ask a wife who is being controlled if there is a problem and she will say, "Absolutely! He needs to stop controlling me!" It's much harder for this same wife to admit that she *allows* herself to be controlled. Ask a controlling husband if there is a problem, and he may be oblivious to the damage his behavior is causing or too insecure to want to see it. Admitting you have a problem in your marriage requires changing your perspective.

Marriage and Niagara Falls

Have you ever been to Niagara Falls? The power and majesty of the falls are absolutely breathtaking. It is a wonderful testament to the majesty of creation. If you take the boat cruise under the Falls, you can feel the immense power of the water. Imagine yourself at the top of Niagara Falls about to go over the edge. There would be no way you could turn yourself around. Once you go over the Falls, there is no turning back.

You may have seen the Falls but have you gone upriver a few miles? You get a different perspective from there; the river is quite calm and peaceful. There is no hint of the roaring descent awaiting the unsuspecting river traveler just a few miles ahead. Upstream, without the power of the Falls to control your movements, you can float in the river or swim to the bank. But as you get closer to the Falls, you begin to see signs of the increasing strength of the water. The current picks up, you have to paddle harder to get out of the current, and at a certain point you can no longer escape the river's power. More signs of approaching trouble appear. A wire cable runs across the river to grab on to as a last resort; signs and flashing lights warn of the danger to come. Soon the sound of the Falls becomes deafening. As you go over the edge, your fate is sealed, and you regret not getting out of the water before it was too late.

Bill Fleeman[1] has applied this analogy to anger management and substance abuse, but it accurately describes control and power issues in marriage as well. In the middle of the churning water, when it seems most hopeless, couples no longer have the ability to prevent the destruction that is coming. Upriver, where the water was calmer, they could have stepped back, looked at their own parts in the conflict, and considered alternatives.

Noelle and Steve had been through this so many times they knew exactly what to expect. It didn't really matter what got them started. It could be an argument over his working too many hours or a discussion about her mother. This particular Saturday morning, it started out innocently enough. Steve was going through the bills and noticed the utility bill didn't show a payment for the previous month.

"Sweetheart, I think they made a mistake on the power bill. They said we didn't pay last month, but you paid that, right?"

Noelle's first response indicated her confidence that she had paid the bill. "Sure, hon, I paid that."

He had heard that before, so he wasn't convinced. "When did you pay it?"

"That same day you gave it to me. I think I did. Yeah, I'm sure I did."

Steve called the utility company, and the lady on the phone assured him that they had not received any payment. He thought to himself, *Here we go again. She didn't pay another bill, and I have to pay another late charge. I'm sick of this!* He paid the bill over the phone, after unsuccessfully trying to get the late charge dropped. His anger was beginning to boil over.

"Noelle," he called. No response. "Noelle!"

"What's up?"

"You didn't pay that bill, did you?"

"Yes, I did. Why?"

"I called the power company. They never got the check."

Noelle looked perplexed. "I was sure I paid that . . ." She went and got her purse, looked through it for a few minutes, and then pulled out a stamped envelope. "I'm sorry, Steve. It's right here. I guess I did forget."

"This happens all the time! I am so tired of paying late fees. It's not rocket science. You promised you'd be more responsible."

"I try, Steve. There's just so much to do, and the boys make it so much harder. You have no idea what I go through every day."

"It's just not that hard, Noelle!" he said, standing up and raising his voice. "You have to learn to organize yourself. This is important! We can damage our credit rating, and these late charges are starting to pile up."

Noelle looked hurt. "You don't have to be mean. I just forgot. It's not like I did it on purpose."

"You always have some excuse. It's getting old. Can't you just fix this?" Steve's voice had continued to get louder. He was close to yelling now, and his tone had taken a nasty turn.

"What do you want from me? I'm doing the best I can!"

Steve began to pull out the big guns. "I just can't depend on you to do what I ask! I don't know why I bother . . ."

Noelle, with tears beginning to pool in her eyes, asked, "Bother with what?"

"Forget it. It wouldn't do any good anyway."

Knowing she would regret it, she kept pushing him. "No, you were thinking it, so go ahead and say it."

"This whole thing. It's just not working. You keep saying you'll change, and you never do."

"Me? What about you, Steve? You promised you'd stop yelling and hurting my feelings. You're doing it again."

"Are you kidding me? You're going to blame this on *me*? Unbelievable. This whole thing tonight would never have happened if you'd just paid the bill like you promised."

"You keep threatening to leave. Why don't you just do it? If I'm such a terrible wife, why don't you just leave?"

"Don't tempt me. Believe me, I might!"

Clearly, Noelle and Steve went over the Falls. There were warning signs everywhere that they should have seen. In this chapter, you will learn to admit that you have a problem, understand how to make the decision to change, and apply the metaphor of Niagara Falls to your marriage.

Seeing the Light

Jan could never understand why someone who promised to love her, professed a Christian faith of compassion and understanding, and came from a wonderful family could treat her the way I did. She didn't realize that I brought plenty of baggage from my past into the marriage. Most important, I had become quite skilled at deflecting responsibility for my own behavior onto others. It was easier to blame Jan, God, my parents, or the cat than it was to accept personal responsibility and face my own inadequacies. I asked God to change me many times, but without my putting in any effort, I was just using God as another excuse not to accept personal responsibility.

I wanted to be better—I tried to be better—but I just kept doing what I wanted. In a letter to the Romans in the Bible, Paul says, "I do not understand what I do. For what I want to do I do not do, but what I hate I do" (Rom. 7:15). There were some days that it seemed no matter how hard I tried, I could never treat Jan the way she deserved. On other days, I just didn't even try that hard.

Three main factors led to my decision to start becoming the husband that Jan deserved: faith, our children, and love. These may not be the same areas you need to look at in your marriage. I just know they were powerful enough to get my attention.

The Power of Faith

My Christian faith provided a standard of behavior for me as a husband, but just knowing that you are supposed to be a certain type of man doesn't necessarily mean you will do what is needed to make that happen. At a certain point in our marriage, my faith created a strong enough feeling of shame and guilt about how I was treating my wife that it was not possible to be satisfied with what I was doing. I began to desire to live up to the standard set by the tenets of my faith.

For change to occur, I believe there has to be a motivating force present that is stronger than your own self-interests, especially if your natural tendency is to think of yourself first. This is why some type of moral, social, or spiritual guidelines are often the motivation needed. Otherwise, even if some change begins to take place, it is usually short-lived. A husband has to believe in something more important than his own desires to seriously consider a model of relationship with his wife that focuses on her before himself.

The Power of Children

One of the most powerful influences in changing the behavior of a husband or wife is their children. I have seen inmates decide to turn their lives around, clients choose to overcome incredible obstacles, and couples choose to transform their marriages, all because of their children. There is something about the desire to do right by our kids that motivates us to change.

Honestly, that was an even more powerful influence for me to change than my faith was. I had been a follower of Christ since I was young, and despite that faith, I hadn't changed. The truth was that I was more interested in meeting my own needs than in pleasing God. This changed one day when I was watching my two boys interact with Jan.

My oldest son was a young teenager and he was telling Jan he wanted to get a video game. Jan told him he would have to wait, because she had some other things she needed to do. Brit became angry and belligerent. He told Jan she wasn't doing anything important and she could run him to the video store. I heard a tone in his voice that scared me. It was almost as if he were ordering her to do something.

At first, I was angry at him and thought *Who do you think you are, kid? You can't talk to your mother that way.* Then I sat back and thought about why he would act that way. It hit me like a ton of bricks. *He learned it from me. I'm teaching my sons not to respect their mother and probably to disrespect all women. How did this happen?*

I didn't say anything at that moment. I was too overwhelmed by the realization that my sons were watching me, soaking up everything I did, and copying my behavior. God used this to remind me very clearly of the hypocrite I was—sitting in the pew in church and professing to love others above myself, while teaching my sons to care more about themselves than their own mother.

There was not an overnight transformation. In fact it has taken many years for me to make some progress in my ability to think of Jan first; this will continue to be something I have to devote myself to every day. However, my wife tells me she was able to see the difference in my behavior during the weeks and months that followed this revelation. It takes time to learn a new behavior and I'm still learning. Often I ask Jan to tell me when things I do contribute to her feeling that I am trying to control her or not listening to her.

The Power of Love and Loss

When you love someone as much as I love my wife, you will do almost anything for her. I say almost because, clearly, I wasn't willing to stop controlling her for many years. That doesn't mean I don't, or didn't, love her. It just means I still cared more about my own needs than those of my wife.

The qualities I love so much about my wife are her kind soul, softness, selflessness, compassion for others, bright spirit, friendship, and her positive outlook on life. She always looks for the best in everyone, despite all she has been through in her life. It takes only a look and a smile from her to completely brighten my day. I have always kidded her that "everybody loves Jan!" and it's true. She has been my friend, my soul mate, and my inspiration and she makes me want to be a better man.

Around the same time that I was beginning to see what a hypocritical Christian I was, as well as understanding that I was teaching my sons to be like me, I also began to realize I was losing Jan. I'm not referring to the "D" word, for over the years I realized she would not ask for a divorce. I was losing the woman I had married because I was crushing her spirit and her soul. I realized that the very thing I was most fearful of—losing her—was happening in front of my eyes. This was what I was trying to prevent by controlling her, so how could I be causing my own worst fears to come true? She might stay married to me but she would not be the same woman I married. To me, that was even worse.

This was the final piece of the puzzle for me. In addition to my poor Christian witness and the revelation that I was training my sons to be just like me, I realized that my behavior was driving my wife away. There was no way I could remain on that path. I had to make a conscious decision to devote myself, every day, for the rest of my life, to becoming the man she deserved to have as her husband.

When I was writing this section, I asked Jan to tell me about her perceptions of this transition in our marriage. She said that early in our marriage she didn't realize what was happening to either of us. She told me, "Your control felt normal to me, because I never knew anything different. I grew up with a father who directed and controlled my life, so I was used to trying to please him and avoid his anger."

When I asked her why she put up with my behavior, she said, "You had so many great qualities in so many other areas; I just focused on all the good things about you. When you have low self-esteem like I have always had, you kind of feel like you deserve to be treated that way." Jan does remember confronting me on our first anniversary and telling me that she felt like a "bird in a gilded cage" and that she didn't want to live that way, without a voice and feeling like a "puppet on a string."

Jan and I have both seen counselors to get help, and I did ask her to go with me to marriage counseling at times. However, she was afraid I would simply manipulate the counselor the way I did her, so she never agreed to go to couple's counseling.

Stopping the Process

I became acquainted with the Niagara Falls metaphor while I was working in the prison system and using Bill Fleeman's material for anger management classes with inmates. In recent years, when I realized how much this metaphor fits marriage, I asked Bill and his organization, Pathways to Peace, to allow me to adapt it for counseling married couples, and they have been kind enough to agree. Many of the couples I have seen over the years have benefited from the application of this metaphor to their marriage, and I have certainly found it to be transformational in my own marriage.

Think of your marriage and the challenges you face in terms of Niagara Falls. When a conflict or a disagreement arises, there are many points at which you and your partner have the opportunity to stop the process before approaching the Falls. It's not as if you haven't seen this movie before. Maybe it starts with a look or a comment that he makes. You feel hurt or offended, and you say something back. One of you may try to stop the fight, but chances are, the other pursues and wants to keep the argument going.

If you keep fighting, you know exactly what will happen. One of you starts to raise your voice and the other ups the ante by bringing up something that happened two years ago. You each know the words to use that will really hurt the other—the places where each of you are sensitive. The more you feel backed into a corner, the more you want to protect yourself. You are almost at the Falls, and soon, you will not be able to stop from moving to threats, in words or actions, that you will never be able to take back.

It doesn't have to be this way. You can stop the process before you get to the Falls. I understand that you want to "win" the fight and prove your point. Right now, you are both more focused on proving you are right than on listening to and understanding each other.

The Niagara Falls metaphor fits nicely with marriage relationships for several reasons. First, many interactions between couples develop progressively, with one disagreement setting the stage for the next. Just like with the increasing power of the river, if you don't deal with the issues when they come up, the conflicts will build on each other with increasing intensity.

Second, marital interactions occur in a family system that puts many pressures on the couple. The force of this pressure is very similar to the power of the Falls and the overwhelming strength that it can present. It may feel like you are stressed all the time and any one conflict can push you over the edge.

Third, just like the Falls, the closer you get to the danger zone, the harder it is to get out of the river. The longer your anger and frustration are allowed to build, the harder it will be to prevent an eventual explosion. It reaches a point when neither of you has the power to turn things around.

Think about the last time you and your spouse had an argument. How many times could you have gotten out of the river and prevented things from getting out of control? From the very first time you realized there was a conflict, there were opportunities to stop the process. Despite the many chances each of you had to walk away, one or both of you kept pushing.

The key to making the Niagara Falls metaphor work for marriage is to identify the warning signs that are unique to your relationship. If you can identify when the conflict is getting out of hand, you can do something to stop it from getting worse. The farther upriver you stop the process, the more options you have. If you can identify the specific behaviors that each of you do that predict when the argument will worsen, you can begin to realize that those behaviors are signals that you need to change course.

Maybe switching metaphors will make this clear. We have some massive snowstorms in Denver, Colorado. If you are in the middle of one of those blinding snowstorms, you have no idea which direction to go for shelter. The whiteout conditions make it impossible to have any frame of reference regarding where you are. When you live here long enough, though, you learn to recognize the signs that a storm is coming. The sky looks different. The air feels different. You know that if you get somewhere safe quickly, you can avoid the worst of it. In marriage, couples need to be aware of the signs that a storm is brewing and get to a safe place before it's too late.

When couples first come to see me, they are often completely unaware of the many warning signs that exist in their relationship. One couple told me that their arguments "just start from nothing" and they were certain there was no way they could see them coming. In a few weeks, we identified at least fifteen warning signs that predicted an oncoming disagreement. These varied from the husband leaving work in a bad mood and the couple's increasing periods without communication, to the wife's strong feeling of fear that things weren't going well and a decrease in sexual activity. They were amazed that there were so many different ways that they could see, hear, and even feel the impending storm.

Making It Personal

In chapter 13, you will learn how you can experience transformation and hope for your marriage as you learn to identify the warning signs of impending danger. You will learn what you can do, right now, to create a better relationship with your spouse, balance power in your marriage, and see results quickly. Then, you will learn how to create change that lasts a lifetime and prevent returning to previous patterns. This will allow you to take the concepts you have learned about "going over the Falls" in your marriage and turn them into real life skills to prevent this from happening.

How many times have you tried to change your husband? You have probably learned, or will soon learn, that you can't do it. Trying to force him to change is setting yourself up for failure. You will likely strike out most of the time, as he has to be the one to decide to change. You may well have learned this lesson and given up trying, just accepting that if you stay married, this is the best it can be. Knowing that you can't make him change does *not* mean that you should stop believing he is capable of change. You can expect change and maintain boundaries and expectations without taking responsibility for making that change happen.

If you give up on your husband, he will certainly give up on himself. I understand that you may be a *giver* and devote much of your life to others' happiness. I have nothing but respect and admiration for women who have developed the ability to think of others before themselves. However, there are limits. When a *giver* is in a relationship with a *taker*, such as a controlling husband, it can lead to a one-way relationship.

The problem is not that you are a loving, caring, devoted wife. That's something you can be proud of. The problem is that marriage is not a one-way street. Both partners have to take care of each other. When you give up on him and stop letting him know what your needs are, you also take away any opportunity for him to change. I realize that it is hard to believe in him when he has let you down so many times before. After all, he started this by not honoring and respecting you, right?

What I want you to understand is that my wife's belief in my ability to change helped me believe in myself. You may assume your husband enjoys controlling you, but if he loves you, I can promise you he doesn't enjoy hurting you. Those two things are mutually exclusive. He needs you to believe he is capable of being the husband you deserve. Underneath his controlling behavior lies a man who is very insecure and wishes he could be different.

To move forward in the transformation of your marriage, you have to begin to expect your husband to succeed. You may have given up hope years ago that he could be *that guy*, but that is part of the problem. You have to believe he is capable of change, hold him accountable for change, and participate in the change with him. Gary Chapman, in *Desperate Marriages*, says that the wife of a verbally abusive husband needs to believe he can be a better man. When she does this, he says, she is "giving him what all of us desperately want—someone to believe in us, someone to believe that we have good characteristics. . . . Since the abuser is already suffering from low self-esteem, such comments build a positive sense of self-worth. . . . he may well return to being the man that you remember."[2]

You may see his controlling behavior as solely his problem. What if rather than a "you" problem or an "I" problem, it is a "we" problem? Some of you may be thinking, *Of course Welch would say that. He's a controlling husband. He's just making excuses for himself and my husband.*

Please hear me. I get that you are hesitant to trust a man who has made the same mistakes your husband has made. However, it is precisely because I have been there that you *can* trust me. I am *not* making excuses for myself or for your husband. I am telling you that I could not have succeeded on this journey without Jan's believing that I was capable of becoming a better man.

Chapman also encourages wives not to "let verbal abuse 'work.' If you give in to your abusive spouse and do whatever the abuser is requesting, you are encouraging the abuse. . . . If you decide not to let these patterns work, you are taking a positive step in breaking the pattern."[3]

I am not asking you to accept his behavior or make excuses for him. I am simply asking you to believe in his ability to change, his love for you, and the power of transformation. If you give up on him, he will most certainly give up on himself. This is how you can help; this is why you can have hope. The road to hope in the future of your marriage begins here. Make a decision right now to take charge of your marriage. You deserve a relationship where respect and love are central, and you can be a part of making that happen.

12

It's Never about
the Can Opener

When we are no longer able to change a situation, we are challenged to change ourselves.

Victor Frankl

"Dr. Welch, I don't want to wait. I want things to get better right now!"

In this chapter, you will learn how to make things better now. I will teach you three specific techniques that you can use to start transforming your relationship immediately. Long-term change takes more time, and we will get into that in depth in the next chapter. Right now, you need to learn how to create positive movement in your relationship. To do this, we need to look at the Rules of Engagement for conflict, identify warning signs that the Falls are near, and learn to see the difference between process and content.

These are skills that you and your spouse need to work on, and I realize your husband may not yet be on board with changing things in the marriage. You should know that many of these things are changes you can begin to create in the relationship without his help. Remember, this process of change is exactly that—a process. He won't suddenly change into Prince Charming overnight. You need to look for small victories—change the things you can change and begin to set boundaries where you can. As he begins to learn there are better, more effective ways of relating to you, change can begin to happen in your marriage.

Noelle and Steve—Remix

Remember Noelle and Steve from the last chapter? After I worked with them for a few months, this couple was able to learn how to recognize the warning signs in their marriage and do things differently. About ten to twelve weeks after they started using the principles you will learn in this chapter, another argument began over a very similar issue. This time, the result was different.

"Noelle, did you pay that gas bill? They say they never got it."

"Of course, Steve. You asked me to."

"Are you sure? They never got it. They charged us a late fee again."

Noelle began to feel attacked. "You know the boys have been sick. I'm trying, Steve. Can you give me a break? I'm doing the best I can. Let's not do this right now."

"This just keeps happening. How many late fees do we have to get before you get organized? I can't do everything myself. I need your help."

"I don't know what happened. Maybe I forgot. I just don't know."

"Noelle . . ."

"Steve, I can't do this right now. I don't want to argue. I know you're mad and I'm sorry but I need a break. I've asked you twice. Please, let's do what the counselor said and take a time-out. We agreed we would both honor that request, right? I need a time-out."

Having to get the last word in, Steve said, "Okay, but we're not done talking about this."

A couple days later, Steve brought it up again. He had calmed down, which helped, but he was still frustrated that they couldn't fix this problem. Noelle was cooking dinner and he confronted her.

"Did you check on that gas bill, Noelle? I've mellowed out. I'm not going to get angry if you didn't pay it. I just need to know. Honestly, you've been doing really well keeping up with all the bills, and we haven't had a late charge in a couple of months. I just need to know."

Noelle was relieved that Steve's tone had changed. He wasn't accusing her. And she was also pleased he had mentioned that she had done really well over the last couple of months with making sure bills were paid.

"I'm not sure if I'm ready to talk about this or not. Are you sure you're not going to get angry? I can't take that right now. You started to get really mad the other night . . ."

"Okay, you may not be ready now but you were supposed to let me know how long I had to wait to discuss it. Remember? It was hard waiting two days without any idea if you would agree to talk about it again or not. You know that it's hard for me to let things go unresolved."

Noelle couldn't argue with that. "Okay, that makes sense. Let's talk about it tonight after dinner when I'm not so rushed."

Steve agreed.

After dinner, they had the kids play a game and they sat down to talk. Noelle reminded Steve he had promised not to get angry, and Steve renewed his promise to remain calm. She told him she had looked at the checkbook and found that she had written the check.

"I think I remember mailing it, Steve, but honestly, with both boys having colds and the weather being so bad, I don't know for sure. I know that this is something I agreed to work on, and until the boys got sick, I was doing pretty well. You even said so earlier."

"Yes, you have done much better. I guess I was hoping that we wouldn't have any more late payments. It creates a lot of stress for me when the bills aren't paid and we get late fees. I know I could pay the bills myself, but this is something you agreed to do for us."

Noelle didn't argue. "I should have told you I wasn't sure if I mailed it the day you asked me about it. I'm sorry I wasn't honest."

Steve admitted that he had let himself get angry very quickly. "I don't know why that bugged me so much. I knew that the boys were sick and you had been doing really well paying bills. I guess I've got a long way to go on this anger control thing. I'm sorry."

Noelle smiled softly and said, "This is going to take a while, isn't it?"

Steve agreed. "No kidding. This isn't easy."

Three Rules of Engagement

To have a fair fight, there have to be rules. A Saturday night bar fight looks a lot different from a prize fight in a ring. Things get completely out of control when there are no rules. It's the same in marriage. There are three Rules of Engagement you need to fight fair.

1. Allow Your Partner to Disengage

The first key in this process is for you and your husband to make an ironclad agreement. Both of you *must* agree that if one of you asks to stop the discussion, the other will not try to force the discussion to continue. I have worked with couples who have chased each other around the house when one partner refused to let the other take a break. In many cases, this happens because the *chaser* doesn't want to "lose" the argument to the *chasee*.

You have to allow your partner space when he or she says it is needed. I've tried pushing Jan to talk when she didn't want to, and I can assure you it does not work. She knows when she needs a break, as we all do. Trying to force the other person into a resolution simply doesn't work, as Steve found out when he tried to force Noelle to keep talking.

2. Make the Time-Out Happen

Once you have committed to honoring each other's request to ask for a break during an argument or disagreement, you need to have a specific process to make this happen. This is harder than you think. The concept isn't difficult to grasp, but the application is.

I suggest that you start by identifying a "safe" phrase. You can use something as simple as "I need a time-out" or "I need a break." It doesn't have to be elaborate; it just has to work. You may want to choose a cute or funny phrase that will break the ice when one of you uses it. Both of you need to agree that when this phrase is used, the discussion is immediately dropped. Neither spouse should try to keep it going, even if the one who asked for the time-out feels guilty about the request. He or she may be quick to give in if the other partner tries to keep the discussion going.

Steve and Noelle had identified a "safe phrase" (I want a time-out), and Steve did eventually honor that (although he should have done so without being sarcastic). You *have* to be able to stop the argument in its tracks and prevent past patterns from recurring. We are primed to respond in the same destructive patterns that we have always used and we can respond before we are even aware of what we are doing.

Choosing to take a time-out is not as easy as it may seem. You have to take your commitment to honor the safe phrase and time-out seriously. In order to stop the argument and give yourself time, you both must stop talking and not have to get the last word in. Most importantly, you have to give up your desire to "win" the argument and be more concerned with positively resolving the disagreement.

In my marriage, when Jan asks for a time-out, I have learned to see this as an opportunity to support Jan and show her love and respect. Jan is asserting her control in the relationship by setting appropriate boundaries. In return, when I honor and respect these requests, I show her that I support her in making healthy choices in our relationship.

3. Return to the Discussion

One of the biggest challenges couples face in this time-out process is that the issue gets dropped completely. The disengagement process cannot become an excuse to avoid conflict or quit on the relationship. For some couples, taking a time-out amounts to running away from the issue. For this strategy to work, the couple has to set a time when the issue will be brought up again.

I have four rules that I suggest to couples regarding this "rescheduling" of the conflict:

1. The person who asked for a time-out must identify a time when he or she will be ready to talk about the problem again.
2. The person who asked for a time-out must identify what was happening that led to the need for a time-out.
3. Both parties have to identify and admit their contribution to the conflict, while also agreeing how they will do things differently the next time.
4. Both parties need to agree that if either is not in the right frame of mind to continue the discussion at the agreed-on time, the discussion will be rescheduled again.

Steve and Noelle did a good job of following all four of these rules when they returned to the discussion. Initially, Steve should have immediately stopped arguing when asked, and Noelle should have given Steve a time when she might be ready to talk again to decrease his anxiety. After that, they did well. When he brought the issue up again, Steve made sure to ask if Noelle was ready to talk about it, and since she wasn't ready, they postponed the discussion again. Both Steve and Noelle owned the mistakes they made during the initial discussion and they were both in a cooperative, unresentful frame of mind when they did talk.

Couples who follow these steps have had very good success at not letting issues drop and making sure resentment doesn't build up. You may have noticed that when issues aren't dealt with in relationships, frustration tends to build up, sometimes resulting in an emotional explosion. It is much better to deal with these conflicts as they arise.

Learning to See the Warning Signs

Understanding how to disengage from an unhealthy process by taking a time-out and gaining control of your emotions is a great start to transforming your marriage. However, to make this work, you have to be able to see the warning signs that trouble is on the horizon. In most cases, these warning signs will be the same regardless of the conflict issue. The following exercise helps couples learn the warning signs that they are approaching the Falls and should turn the boat around while they still can.

Step One: Choose a significant conflict in which, as a couple, you went *over the Falls*. This would be a conflict when you each said things you regretted, one or both of you got very angry, or the argument became destructive and hurtful. Choose an incident that happened recently enough that you both remember your thoughts, feelings, and experiences.

Step Two: Both parties make their own list of every factor that could have contributed to the start of the conflict. This could include thoughts, emotions, state of mind, previous conflicts, and other people that were involved. Or it could be memories of previous problems that this issue brought up, how tired you were, how hungry you were, or even the attitude that your guinea pig, Winston, gave you that morning.

Step Three: Still working individually, rank the importance of each factor. Give everything a rank number, even if some are difficult to rank. The goal here is to get a clear idea of which factors contributed the most to the conflict.

Step Four: Now it's time to start working together again. Share your lists with each other and see what patterns emerge. You will likely see several factors that both of you listed but you will probably be surprised by some things that you hadn't thought of that your partner considered a factor in the conflict. Look over the rankings each of you gave the factors. Talk about things you both ranked high, as these may be important warning signs. Ask each other who would be most likely to see these factors first and warn the other.

Step Five: Finally, as a couple, create a Top Ten list of the warning signs you both saw. Rank them from 1—being a sign of immediate danger of going over the Falls—to 10—being less dangerous. I suggest that you do this by drawing a "river map," an illustration of a river leading to a falls, with each warning sign written in, the most dangerous signs located right before the falls and less dangerous signs located upriver. The goal is to create something you can both refer to in the future to help remind each other of when you are approaching danger.

This exercise creates a map that will help you recognize warning signs that have existed in your relationship. It doesn't matter what the fight is about. You now have a very powerful alarm system that is set to go off when there is impending conflict. You should post this map in a prominent place. If you both pay attention to the warning lights and sirens, the system will alert you in almost any conflict of the danger ahead and the need to get out of the water.

Learning to See the Process Not the Content

There is one more concept that I believe you can implement right now that will begin the process of transformation in your marriage. Over the years, I have come to realize that couples focus way too much on the topic of their disagreement rather than on the way they treat each other. I call this *content versus process*.

Content

Content is the topic that you and your spouse are disagreeing about. It could be something small, like the color of the new carpet or where to have dinner. It could also be something huge, like whether you will move to Boston for his new job or whether or not to have another child. Regardless of how important the topic is, focusing on the content means focusing on the details of the issue itself.

For most of the couples who walk into my office, this is where they live. They fight over who gets their way over the issue *du jour*. In some cases, clients tell me that halfway through an argument, they actually forget what they have been arguing about. You might think that if they don't even remember the reason the fight began, they would give up and call a truce. However, most couples tell me that doesn't slow the fight down at all, for the argument that was set in motion by the initial disagreement seems to have taken on a life of its own.

Therapists spend entire sessions trying to work out solutions to specific problems. Brief counseling and solution-focused therapy have this goal. The problem with this approach is that it is hard to apply what you learn to the next conflict. When a couple solves one problem in a formal setting with a counselor, they don't learn how to resolve conflicts on their own. Even if they do develop some skills, the skills may not translate into solutions for future issues.

Process

In contrast to the problem focus of a content-oriented intervention, focusing on the *process* involves being more concerned with the messenger than the message. How you respond to your partner, whether you create anger and resentment during the discussion, and how honored and respected each partner feels after the interaction are the focus of this approach. Caring about your spouse is much more important in process-focused communication than coming up with a resolution to the problem.

This comes at a cost. If you remain focused on getting your way, then you can't see the other person's point of view or consider their feelings during the argument. You have to choose between proving you are right or making sure your partner's feelings are not hurt, as it may not be possible to do both. The more you try to prove your point to your spouse, the harder it becomes to make sure you prioritize his or her feelings and beliefs.

Process refers to all aspects of the interactions between a couple during a disagreement. This includes the way each partner treats the other during the discussion, how well partners listen to each other, and the emotions that are created by the interaction. The way both spouses feel after the discussion is over and the state of the relationship are much more important than the issue itself.

If you begin to integrate this process into your communication with each other, you will see almost instantaneous results. You will find you remain calmer, see what is happening more clearly, and treat each other better. You may even stop being concerned with who is right or wrong.

The best part is, once you learn this skill, it works for *every topic* you may argue about! The content doesn't matter anymore. You will soon find yourself talking more about your relationship and less about issues that didn't really matter in the first place.

The Can Opener

Every semester I start my Marriage and Family class by showing a clip from an episode of *Everybody Loves Raymond* called "The Can Opener." This show is about Ray, a sportswriter, and his wife, Deborah, who live across the street from his parents and his brother.

In this episode Ray and Deborah tell their very different views of a fight they had the night before.

Ray's account of the story (to his mother) is that he walked into the house and kissed Deborah passionately, asking her to tell him about her day. She dismissed him, just saying that she was fine. Ray asked about dinner, and Deborah replied that she was too tired to make dinner and would get to it later. Ray lovingly replied, "I'll be happy to make my own dinner!" He searched through the cabinets and found a can of tuna fish, stating loudly, "Yum, tuna fish!"

While Ray was searching for a can opener, Deborah explained that she had bought a new one. Ray couldn't figure out how to use it, spilled tuna fish juice, and then dropped the entire can of tuna fish into the sink. He smiled brightly and said, "I would have rather had it on bread, but tuna fish is just as good right out of the sink!" Ray finished the story by saying to his mother, "And I'm not exaggerating at all!"

In stark contrast, Deborah recounted (to Ray's jealous brother, Robert) that Ray walked into a chaotic house with kids running everywhere. Ray ignored her attempts to tell him about her day, instead demanding, "Where's dinner?" Deborah told him, "I haven't had time yet, Ray. If you can just wait a minute . . ." Ray retorted, "Fine! I'll make my own dinner, as usual." Ray began opening cabinet doors and then slamming them shut. He eventually found a can of tuna fish and said sarcastically, "Great! Tuna fish."

Ray threw utensils all around the drawer searching for a can opener, while Deborah explained that she had purchased a new, safer one. Ray tried to use the new can opener but spilled a drop of tuna juice on his finger. He yelled, "Oh, no, tuna juice!" Running to the sink, he dropped the entire can of tuna in the sink then turned menacingly to Deborah and asked, "Did we need a new can opener? What was wrong with the old one?"

When Deborah asked if she could help, Ray said sarcastically, "Gee, I don't know. I would have preferred the tuna fish on bread, but I'm sure it's just as good *right out of the sink*!" Feeling hurt and misunderstood, Deborah started crying and meekly stated, "This can opener is better. It's not stupid, and . . . I'm . . . not . . . stupid . . ."

It's never about the can opener. Ray and Deborah could have been arguing about the laundry or a new job or the in-laws. It really doesn't matter what the issue is in your relationship. What matters is how you talk to each other about the problem, how you treat each other while you are dealing with it, and how respected and heard each partner feels afterward.

Choosing Process over Content

Deciding to change *how* to handle conflict rather than focusing on whatever the current issue is will have a profound effect on your marriage. It is similar to the biblical principle of teaching a man to fish rather than providing fish to eat—teaching the skill lasts a lifetime. It may be necessary to take a time-out to change your focus from yourself to your spouse.

There are some things you can do to take the focus off the issue and on to your spouse. First, you can ask yourself what the end game really is—do you want to win the argument or do you want to have a loving relationship with a spouse who knows you value her? Focusing on content leads to winning arguments, focusing on process leads to a marriage based on love and respect.

Second, you will be much more successful at focusing on process if you don't say anything until you have time to choose your words carefully. The faster you respond, the more likely it will be that it will be content-related. Take your time and think about the effect your words will have on your spouse before you say anything.

Third, when you do say something, start with a statement like "I want you to know my primary concern is that we treat each other with kindness and love while we talk about our differences of opinion." This makes it much more likely that you will focus on your spouse's needs rather than your own.

Despite how overwhelming some of the conflicts you face may be, you do *not* have to remain helpless and hopeless. Your relationship is not hopelessly out of control; you have simply let issues of power and control run the ship, rather than steering it yourself. Now that you have learned to use Rules of Engagement for conflicts, to identify warning signs that you may be heading for the Falls, and to focus on process rather than content, you can use these skills right now to transform your marriage.

Part Five

The Transformational Model of Marriage

Changing Your Marriage for a Lifetime

13

Transforming Your Marriage for a Lifetime

The closest to being in control we will ever be is in that moment that we realize we're not.

Brian Kessler

The key to lifelong marriage transformation is choosing a model of marriage that encourages you to focus on the needs and concerns of your spouse. The principles on which your marriage is based, the reasons you are married, and whom you are serving in the marriage will largely determine the quality of the marriage. I believe that long-term change in a marriage requires commitment to a set of principles that focuses on your partner and not yourself. However, this is not the model of marriage that society values.

Marriage has become a self-focused institution—something to do for your own happiness. You can see this clearly in the media messages we receive every day. There appear to be three major components to the current model of marriage. Here they are: getting your needs met, being happy, and changing partners if this relationship doesn't provide you with the first two.

Tim Keller, in his recent book *The Meaning of Marriage*, states that "marriage used to be a public institution for the common good, and now it is a private arrangement for the satisfaction of the individual. Marriage used to be about us, but now it is about me."[1] I couldn't agree more.

The Me-First! Model of Marriage

Me First! Goal 1: Get My Needs Met

The media tells us to find the person who "meets our needs." According to the Online Dating Statistics website,[2] 40 million Americans have tried online dating, with 20 million eHarmony members and 15 million Match.com members. These sites make their living off their ability to match people based on answers to questions about what they want in a relationship partner. Look at the massive lists of questions that these sites utilize. Most of the questions refer to things we would like to have in a spouse rather than what we need. The prevailing societal model of marriage encourages us to focus on getting our wants met through a checklist of qualifications.

Marital satisfaction is a laudable goal. If you get what you need from your partner, it makes sense that you would want to stay married. The question becomes whether marital satisfaction is based on getting what we want, getting what we need, or giving our partner what he or she wants or needs. We'll look at the first two here and the last one later in the chapter.

WHAT WE NEED

We *need* to feel safe. No relationship thrives if there is fear of harm or some threat present. That's what went so wrong in my relationship with my wife. She did not feel safe being who she was or expressing her feelings because of the irrational ways I responded. Safety and security are basic human needs. When someone controls you by exercising power over you, it can make you feel unsafe.

We *need* to be loved and accepted. In Western society, couples almost universally say they got married because they "fell in love." Whether what they feel is actually love is open for debate, but the *feeling* of being in love seems to be a prerequisite for getting married in our culture. For that feeling of being in love to exist, we must feel accepted by our mate for who we are.

We *need* to be honored and respected. I see this over and over again in my marriage counseling practice. Whether it is due to an affair, working too much, recreational activities, or simply different priorities, couples struggle mightily when one partner does not feel respected or honored. Each partner must believe he or she is valued by the other.

We *need* to have a shared understanding of meaning and purpose in life. Couples may have differences in levels of faith and religious beliefs but they need to have compatible purposes that provide meaning to their life. When a couple's religious and faith journeys are significantly different, it can cause great difficulty in making major life decisions. Couples need to agree, at least in principle, on why they were placed on this earth and what their purpose in life is.

What We Want

We *want* to be happy. We *want* to be taken care of. We *want* to be financially secure. We *want* to be sexually satisfied. We *want* to have a lot of things, but we don't *need* them. We can debate what should be on the list of genuine needs in relationships. However, I would suggest that things you might want, other than the needs I listed above, are simply *wants*, not *needs*. If marital partners feel safe, loved and accepted, honored and respected, and share a purpose and meaning in life, most other things take care of themselves.

Me First! Goal 2: Don't Worry! Be Happy!

The old Bobby McFerrin song, "Don't Worry! Be Happy!" could be the theme song for the prevailing model of marriage today. Where did we get the expectation that happiness in life (and in marriage) was a right that we all deserve? People assume that if they are not happy, someone needs to change to accommodate them. The unchecked narcissism that seems so pervasive in current American culture was not always our societal value. In fact, only a couple of generations ago, people were much more focused on helping others, did not expect to get handouts (often turning them down), and were much less self-centered.

It may be that a couple of generations of children who were pampered and coddled have now brought to marriage a new set of expectations. Children who grew up getting a trophy just for participating in athletic events now as adults expect things to be handed to them. This air of entitlement is much more prevalent today than in previous generations.

Couples who are successful in maintaining lifelong marriages develop the capacity to be satisfied in the relationship regardless of what part of the roller-coaster track they are on. They don't settle for the depth of the low points and they work hard to get out of them, but they also don't give up and end the relationship when they are not constantly at the high points. Like a roller coaster, marriage has its ups and downs.

Me First! Goal 3: Trade Up if You Need To

There is a phenomenon in the United States now known as the "starter marriage," a phrase coined by Pamela Paul[3] that seems to be quite popular with the Millennial generation. The concept of a starter home, which couples buy and live in for a few years until trading up to a nicer one, is applied to marriage, with an expectation of trading up to a better relationship when one partner wants to. The first marriage is just a place to get your feet wet, figure out what you really want, and then trade up (once or twice) until you find the dream marriage you have always wanted. The concept is popular enough that there was even a recent TV show titled *The Starter Wife.*

This new version of marriage reminds me of a client who compared the affair he had to buying a new car. You remember how amazing your current car looked on the showroom floor. It had all the bells and whistles when you bought it. It's been a few years now, and she doesn't look or drive the way she used to. There are some dents in the fenders, the new car smell and shine are gone, and it takes her longer to get started in the morning (of course, she would probably say the same thing about you!). You notice you are beginning to look at new cars around you a bit more than you used to. And just yesterday you were admiring that beautiful new car that pulled up next to you at the stoplight. Trading in your old, beat-up car starts to look like a pretty good choice.

You see where I'm going, don't you? We're not talking about cars anymore. Whether you are a disillusioned wife who starts seeing other men in her life as a significant step up from her controlling husband or a frustrated husband who finds himself looking at other women in a sexual light, you are playing with fire. Your level of frustration with your current marriage makes you a high risk for an affair, a divorce, or both.

The Transformational Model of Marriage

Pay close attention to this next section. If truly transformational change is to occur in your marriage, you *must* understand this point very clearly. Until now, you have probably seen this book as written primarily to you and for you as the wife of a controlling husband. This is where things begin to change. For real change to occur in your marriage you cannot simply rely on your husband to change—*you* have to be willing to change also.

In the next four chapters of this book, you will learn about the four principles of Transformational Marriage—*praise, hope, forgiveness,* and *selflessness.* You will learn how each of these four principles has a tremendous effect on how power and control are handled in marriage. This model differs significantly from the prevailing model of marriage in America. Transformational Marriage prioritizes your spouse over yourself and it requires both of you to buy into this type of relationship. Your own needs become secondary to those of the person with whom you have chosen to share your life, so you always have each other's back.

These chapters will focus on your relationship and how *both* of you need to change. You may have spent much of your marriage blaming your husband for his behavior, and he does deserve a great deal of the blame. Here's the point—you have had your part in the relationship turning out as it has too. You tacitly agreed to be controlled by refusing to set boundaries on his behavior. Perhaps you developed a pattern of doing whatever was necessary to avoid confronting your husband to keep him happy and avoid conflict. You may also have not been honest with your husband and kept your feelings to yourself. You may even have blamed yourself for his behavior rather than holding him accountable for it.

One of the cornerstones of the Transformational Marriage process is accepting the fact that patterns that develop in marriage involve both partners. As you read this, you may feel offended—*Come on, Welch. Are you seriously blaming me for his behavior?* That is not my intention. However, I do believe you have your part in encouraging, allowing, or accepting his controlling behavior. One of the most important steps you can take in beginning the process of change is to accept that both partners have to choose to do life together differently for permanent change to occur in a marriage.

This may be hard for you to accept. I am just asking you to keep an open mind to this possibility as you read the next few chapters. Maybe your husband deserves 90 percent of the blame; maybe it's more like 60/40. I don't know. I just know that in my marriage and in those of the couples I work with, both partners have to agree to accept some responsibility for what has taken place in the past in order to work as a team to change things in the future.

Even if your husband doesn't show any interest in changing, these next four chapters can help you begin the process of change.

Introducing praise to your relationship can soften your husband's responses and begin to create hope in the future of the marriage. In addition, when a couple is able to begin to forgive each other, a controlling husband has the opportunity to change his behavior and begin to treat you the way you deserve to be treated. Most importantly, the transformational marriage process can help you transform your relationship into a marriage based on selflessness rather than selfishness. When this occurs, controlling husbands gain the ability to focus on their wives' needs before their own, and your relationship will never be the same.

The most important key to changing your marriage is choosing to care more about your spouse than about yourself. Your care for your spouse is evident every day in the way you communicate. If you don't care about your spouse more than yourself, all the communication skills and counseling in the world won't do any good. The first key to unlocking the challenges you are facing in your marriage is for both of you to make each other a higher priority than your being right.

Think about the reasons your husband needs to win arguments with you. What purpose does winning serve? He may want to win arguments with his friends or co-workers, although the need to be right in those situations is suspect too. But when the person he claims to love and cherish is involved, the game changes. It took me a long time to learn this lesson. I wasted way too much time proving points to my wife and intimidating her just to win arguments. In the end the only thing I accomplished was making Jan feel of less value than me, leaving her feeling discouraged and less likely to share her opinions in the future.

This is one of the insidious little secrets about power and control in marriage. What really happens when a husband controls his spouse is that she is simply less likely to talk to him in the future (at least about important things). The husband's need for control builds a barrier between him and his partner. When he does this, he shuts down his wife, telling her how wrong she is, talking over her, and generally making her feel useless. Why would she share her personal opinions with someone who is going to cut her down and make her feel bad?

Contrast that with choosing to understand the other person, investing effort to make the other person feel listened to and heard, and prioritizing the relationship and each other's feelings above winning the argument. What a different experience that would be for a couple! Neither partner would get their way all the time, they wouldn't necessarily end up with the "best" decision every time, and they might not even feel that their point of view was fairly heard. But when building up the relationship and loving each other become more important than being *right*, transformation takes place.

Transformational Communication for a Lifetime

Transformational Communication involves an entirely new way of communicating with each other. This process takes time, it will feel uncomfortable, and it is hard. You have to commit to following all the steps and trusting the process. (In chapter 18 I will offer specific advice for encouraging your husband to participate if he is reluctant to change.) It will become easier and feel more comfortable the more you do it. I believe that if you as a couple give this process a chance, communication between you will be radically changed in ways you never thought possible. Learning to communicate in this way will set the stage for the other lifelong changes you will learn to make.

Step 1: Communication Ground Rules

You need to talk about *how* you want to talk to each other before you actually do it, even if that means delaying the discussion as you learned to do in the chapter on taking time-outs. Setting up rules that you both agree to follow is extremely important, and if either partner stops following these rules, the conversation should end. You should both agree that if one partner doesn't follow the rules, you will use the time-out process you learned earlier to take a break. You should return to the conversation only when you both agree to follow the rules. Here are ten rules for communication I suggest, but you can certainly come up with your own.

10 Rules for
Transformational Relationship Communication

1. Respect and honor your partner in all you say and do.
2. Focus on the communication process instead of the content.
3. Let the past stay in the past.
4. Avoid early-morning or late-night discussions.
5. Think about how your partner will hear what you plan to say.
6. Speak in bullet points (short statements that clearly make your point).
7. Listen to *all* of what your partner says.
8. Restate what your partner says to show that you heard it correctly.
9. Avoid bunny trails (stick to the topic at hand).
10. Leave third parties out of the conversation (don't refer to others' opinions—just your own).

Step 2: The Wife Gets to Speak First

The communication style I recommend is called intentional reflective listening. The basic format for such communication has three parts: listening to what the other person has to say, restating it, and responding to it. I learned a great deal about this type of focused reflective listening from watching Harville Hendrix and Helen Hunt demonstrate these techniques at a workshop a few years ago. Their book, *Getting the Love You Want*,[4] has some excellent exercises for practicing these skills. Though I don't share all of their views on how marriage works, their advice on how to communicate with intentional reflective listening is excellent. The reflective listening skills described here are based partly on the work of Hendrix and Hunt, although many others have used this approach in the past.

The entire purpose of communicating has to change for a controlling husband. It can no longer be to convince his wife that he is right. If he starts by immediately trying to get his point across, the balance of power is already messed up. To increase the likelihood that both points of view will be heard, the wife should speak first, especially if she is the one with the concern. So after the ground rules are set, the wife should speak about the concern at hand.

Step 3: The Husband Restates

Before the husband responds to what his wife has said, he restates what he has understood her to say. Think about the conversations you have had in the past year. When was the last time you spoke with someone and you left the conversation absolutely convinced they totally understood you—that they *got you?* This is an extremely powerful experience that we rarely have.

Restating what you understand back to the other person is an honoring gesture, as it is almost impossible for your spouse to miss the fact that you are interested in their point of view and that you get what they are trying to say to you. If the husband gets something incorrect in what he restates, the wife clarifies and corrects what he missed, and he continues to restate until he gets exactly what his wife wanted him to understand.

Step 4: The Husband Responds

The husband does *not* get to criticize or analyze what his wife said, as that is not the purpose of the conversation. However, he can share his thoughts and feelings about what she said if she is ready to listen to him. This usually is more successful after the husband has taken some time to process what was said. He should not try to convince her she is wrong.

When his wife feels ready to listen fully to her husband's response to what she shared, he tells her his thoughts and feelings on the subject. She listens and then she follows step 3, restating what she understands that her husband said. If she doesn't get it right, her husband makes clarifications and she restates what he said. This continues until she gets it right. Then she follows step 4 and responds to what he said. As with her husband, she cannot criticize or analyze what she has heard.

Step 5: The Action Plan

By this point, both parties have a clear understanding of what the other is thinking and feeling. It is now possible to discuss honestly and respectfully what can be done about the issue. As they work through ideas and suggestions, they may need to follow the reflective listening process, with each listening to the other and restating what they hear. Couples can adapt the process as they become better at listening to each other, and sometimes the rules are relaxed depending on the topic and the couple's interactions. The primary goal for each person is to listen to the other and to feel they have been heard clearly and accurately.

A Concluding Thought

If you remember to focus on the person you say you love and cherish, then the issue that you felt you had to fight about suddenly loses its power. The key is learning to respond to each other in positive ways that decrease conflict, rather than following that old, familiar negative path you've been down before. Focusing on the process of how you treat each other, rather than the often trivial issue that started the argument, can help you appreciate the unique qualities of your spouse, rather than resenting the differences.

14

Praising Each Other

Building Up instead of Tearing Down

Too often we underestimate the power of a touch, a smile, a kind word, a listening ear, an honest compliment, or the smallest act of caring, all of which have the potential to turn a life around.

Leo Buscaglia

In 1992 John Gottman began a ten-year study of couples to see if he could predict those who would stay married. With 94 percent accuracy, he found that he could predict which couples would stay married based on what has been called his "magic ratio" of five positive actions for every one negative.[1] This shows how incredibly powerful negative statements are and that their influence is multiplicative. Making three or four negative comments is like giving up three touchdowns in the first quarter. You are so far behind in the score, it is almost impossible to catch up. We are too quick to correct our partners and complain about them, while we rarely tell them how special, unique, and loved they are.

In our marriage, Jan is much more supportive than I am, either by nature or by choice. I have a tendency to critique first and ask questions later. It would be a cop-out to blame this on either my gender or my personality. I need to take responsibility for my choices.

Jan has taught me that harsh words stay with each of us long after the words are said. If I don't filter myself, I have a tendency to say what I think without considering the effect of my words. I remember my mother trying to teach this to me as a young man, but this was not a lesson I chose to learn. Seeing the effect that my negative comments have had on Jan over the years, I have worked diligently to consider the words I use before I open my mouth.

The controlling husband is especially prone to criticism, so this chapter is vital in helping him learn to replace this with praise. When he begins to see that he can get his own needs met much more efficiently with praise than complaints, he can learn that his controlling behavior is not the only way to achieve his goals. Integrating praise into a controlling marriage can be the first step in lasting change.

"Danger, Will Robinson!"

For some, the phrase "Danger, Will Robinson!" brings back memories of *Lost in Space*, either the original TV version or the 1998 big screen version. When the robot (whom the creative writers saw fit to name "Robot") boomed out, "Danger, Will Robinson!" we were all on edge, waiting for what would come next. We prepared ourselves for seeing Will in danger. Unfortunately, the warning signs that we are in danger of saying something we will regret are not as clear as Robot's metallic voice.

Nonetheless, we are capable of learning to see the danger signals and take action. For me, signals that I may be in danger of saying something insensitive are things like lack of sleep, frustration with or tiredness from work, time deadlines, and emotionally charged topics. I can almost guarantee that without intervention, I am much more likely to say something I will regret under these conditions.

The key is identifying these risk factors and taking action before you engage your spouse in a discussion.

The good news is that you have already learned the Niagara Falls metaphor techniques that are so valuable in these situations. In chapter 12 you learned how to identify the warning signs in your relationship so that you can prevent an argument before it happens. If you read chapter 11 carefully and applied it to your relationship, you should have already identified many of your triggers, which are the actual events that get an argument started.

You can prevent many conflicts by agreeing to give each other some space when you both first get home from work. I tell couples to start out by praising each other when they walk in, sharing a hug and kiss, and then giving each other a half hour of decompression time before they *enter the family*. I have seen this work especially well with military and law enforcement families, as the stress and pressure of the work environment usually demand this buffer period.

A while back, I made this suggestion to a couple who were struggling with this issue. The wife's response was very direct. "He doesn't need that time. He already has a thirty-minute drive home to calm down and relax before he sees us." Her husband beat me to the response I was prepared to give, confirming my expectations. "Driving home is insane. The traffic raises my stress level, and I'm way more tense when I walk in the door." If you start with praise and positive interactions, followed by some downtime, the evening will go much better.

Empowering Your Spouse

The first aspect in transforming your marriage is learning to praise. We should build up the person we marry, not tear them down! However, praising others is not what we are trained to do. From an early age, kids are told what to do by parents, teachers, and coaches. Once we get a job, our boss tells us what to do, and no matter how high we climb the corporate ladder, there always seems to be someone above us giving orders. Shouldn't our marriages be places of safety where we can be loved and appreciated rather than criticized?

Willard Harley discusses how his Love Bank concept applies to praise and criticism in *Effective Marriage Counseling*. Harley says that "love units" are deposited through praise and withdrawn through criticism. "Almost everything a husband and wife do affects each other positively or negatively, and that effect determines the feelings they have for each other. If they affect each other positively enough and avoid affecting each other too negatively, they will be in love with each other."[2]

When a wife feels unappreciated and criticized by her husband, she may choose to stay married but quit investing in the relationship, giving up hope that her husband will ever be the husband she hoped he would be. In many ways, not investing in your marriage is as much a decision to quit on the relationship as is choosing to get a divorce. Either choice makes transformation in the relationship unlikely. A better alternative is for a wife to focus on empowering her husband to change and creating a climate that encourages this. Jack and Judith Balswick refer to the process of praising one another as "empowerment." In their words, "mutual empowerment is a reciprocal process of building up, equipping, supporting, encouraging, affirming, and challenging." They believe that this process allows a husband and wife to collaborate in a mutual process of sharing power as a couple.[3]

Choosing to empower your spouse, instead of criticizing, critiquing, and cutting them down, can change your life and that of the one you love. John Gottman has long been regarded as a pioneer in the field of marital research. His work is based on years of research with couples in his marital lab. One of his seminal concepts is The Four Horsemen: criticism, contempt, defensiveness, and stonewalling. These, he says, are present in destructive relationships.[4]

Although Gottman might not agree, I have always felt that these concepts develop progressively. In the couples I work with, criticism starts a destructive downward spiral. When critical comments be-come acceptable, the stage is set for feelings of disrespect and contempt. When criticism becomes commonplace and contempt sets in, it is no surprise that the partner being criticized begins to withdraw and becomes very defensive. It's like a prize fighter retreating to the safety of his corner for protection—it's human nature. Finally, what Gottman calls stonewalling occurs, when partners completely disengage from each other and the door to communication is slammed shut.

Changing criticism to praise, or even just eliminating criticism, can be an entry point for a husband who is refusing to go to coun-seling or is completely disinterested in looking at how much he controls you. Talk to him about making this one change in your relationship—stop the criticism. Even if replacing criticism with praise seems to be an impossible dream, just stopping the criticism is a great place to start.

My mother taught me something that her mother taught her. I can hear her as clearly as if she were standing right here. "Ron, if you don't have something good to say, don't say anything at all." There is a tremendous amount of wisdom in that advice. This might be the best first step you can take toward transforming your marriage.

Changing our human tendency to criticize is not easy, as it is grounded in our tendency to be selfish. We notice the things that we don't like before things we do like. You may have to remind yourself to focus on the positive until it becomes a habit.

There are people who work hard to be positive and tell others what they are doing well. However, these people are clearly the exception not the rule. For most of us, this is a skill we have to practice extensively to have any hope of mastering.

Criticism is just another word for correction. If there is a lot of correcting going on in your relationship, you need to ask yourself why this is happening. When did it become okay for one or both of you to find fault with the other? There was a time when you built each other up and told each other how wonderful you each were. Has something changed, or do you take each other for granted now? You need to assess what is happening in the relationship and how you got here.

So Now What?

It would be great if you and your spouse both decided to make praise and empowerment a way of life. However, you can initiate some changes on your own, even if your spouse isn't on board yet. Someone has to make the first move, right? It might as well be you. Sometimes, it doesn't take a dramatic confrontation for transformation in a relationship to start. One person can simply decide to be different. Whether it is just you or you and your partner, here are some steps you can take to start the process of making praise a daily part of your relationship.

Step 1: Stop and Consider How Your Spouse Will Respond

The first step in learning to praise your spouse is to stop and think about the person you are talking to and how he or she will feel if you say what you plan to say. This is not that hard to do if you discipline yourself. In fact when you are talking about the person you love, the real question is why you would even consider criticizing instead of praising. Doesn't it make more sense to focus on building your spouse up and helping him or her feel good?

Before you criticize your spouse, it will help to think, very specifically, about how the words you are about to say will make your spouse feel. It isn't enough to just think about how *you* would feel if someone said this to you. You aren't saying it to yourself. You have to think about how your spouse will feel. Whether you have been married three months, three years, or thirty years, you know enough to predict your spouse's response.

This is where pressure, stress, and emotional intensity can create problems. It is harder to make yourself stop and think about the consequences of your words when you are too angry to think clearly or under time pressure to deal with something immediately. You need to be aware of the triggers that can make it hard for you to be patient and take the time to stop and consider the effect of your words.

Step 2: Say It Another Way

Assuming that you have found a way to slow things down long enough to consider how your spouse will feel if you say what you plan on saying, ask yourself two questions:

1. Do I really need to say this at all?
2. If I really do need to say this, is there another way I can say it that will build up my spouse instead of tearing him or her down?

When a husband is critical of his wife, she can ask her husband to think about what he wants his criticism to accomplish. If his goal is to get you to do what he wants, ask him to consider changing his goal to helping you feel good about yourself. He has to get used to thinking about his purpose before he says things, and this will likely be a new experience for him. If you accept my premise that he wishes he could learn a different way to treat you, he may be much more open to this than you expect.

Your husband needs to consider what he knows about you as a person, how you have reacted in the past, and how you will likely react now. If he wants you to hear him, he needs to speak in a way that will encourage you to listen. You can help him see the wisdom in approaching you this way. Let him try to say what he means in different ways, without judging his attempts. If it is still hurtful, ask him to try again.

From my years of work with clients and my experience in my own marriage, I have become convinced of the value of qualifying statements. By this I mean statements such as, "I may be completely wrong, but . . ." or "I want you to know I am aware this can be a sensitive topic for you, so if what I say begins to feel hurtful, please stop me." These statements are called *qualifiers* and they set the stage for what is to be said. When you make statements that show you are thinking about your spouse's feelings, it is much easier for your spouse to respond positively.

Step 3: Unmistakable Acts of Kindness

Once you have succeeded in learning to stop and think before speaking, as well as developing the ability to restate the thoughts in more respectful and honoring ways, you can go to the third step in the praise and empowerment process. Working on the words you use with your spouse is more important than this last step, because, contrary to the old adage, *words speak louder than actions*. But that does not mean that actions are unimportant. Unmistakable acts of kindness can reinforce the positive things that have been said.

I am not talking about things like buying anniversary gifts, which are expected. I am talking about doing things that are intentionally meant to make your partner feel special. A husband can take his wife out to dinner to show her that he appreciates her, but if he does this on her birthday, she files it under "really nice birthday." There is almost no chance that it gets filed under "He thinks I'm an amazing person" or "Wow! He makes me feel great about myself." For your spouse to hear this message, these things have to be done for no reason other than to show your spouse how important, valuable, and generally awesome he or she is. The now famous book *The Love Dare*[5] is filled with examples of daily steps you can take to send loving messages to your partner.

These actions don't have to take a lot of time, and some can become habits, repeated over and over. Many years ago, Chick-Fil-A started handing out small, stuffed cows as a promotion for their "Eat More Chikin" advertising campaign. Jan and I ended up with a bunch of those cows. One day, Jan put one in my lunch bag with a note that said, "Wanted you to know I'm thinking about you." I got a kick out of that, especially since it was a surprise. I hid the cow under her pillow and, when she found it, I told her I wanted her to know I loved her and was thinking about her.

That began an interchange between the two of us that has continued. We hide the cows in the most unexpected places: in shoes, purses, pillows, computer bags, and anywhere else we can think of. I even find cows in my suitcase when I travel! It is our way of doing a small thing that sends the unmistakable message, "I love you and I appreciate you."

The message comes across even stronger when you personalize what you do to highlight a specific thing that you value about your spouse. For instance, you could create a banner that you hang above the door to your house that says, "You are an amazing husband!" But how much more powerful would it be if it said, "You are incredibly smart, amazingly kind, and truly talented!" Identifying specific areas of your husband's character or abilities can really make the message hit home.

Another way I have found to build Jan up is to keep a "gratitude journal." I haven't had the discipline to do this all of our marriage, but I have found that it is extremely rewarding to her when I give her these journals. This is something either partner can do. All you have to do is buy a journal from your local bookstore and commit to writing in it for fifteen minutes every day. There may be some days you miss, but plan on writing in it every day if you can. Your goal is to write down everything you can think of that you appreciate about your spouse that you have noticed since you last made an entry.

These journals aren't meant to go down in history as examples of literary excellence. I know what I wrote didn't always make perfect sense. I wanted to write from the heart and get down as many thoughts about what I appreciated as I could. It can be very effective to do this as a surprise, save up a few months' worth of writings, and then give them to your spouse as a gift. The one thing you can be sure of is that your spouse can't miss the message that you appreciate and honor all that he or she is and does.

A Final Thought

The great thing about praise is that you don't have to wait for your partner to do this—you can start making this change on your own. In fact, even if your husband is just beginning to consider that he might need to make some changes in the marriage, you can start the process by introducing the idea of praise instead of criticism into the relationship. We have learned over the years that positive behavior leads to partners responding in kind. Even if you don't see immediate reciprocation from you husband, you can feel good about the person you are becoming. Rest assured that he will notice the difference and can learn from the changes you are making.

Start today by making a commitment to say, out loud and often, all the things you appreciate and love about the person you are spending your life with. Build your partner up instead of tearing her or him down. Your spouse will feel more loved, you will feel better about yourself, and your marriage will be transformed.

15

Finding Hope in Each Other

Believing It Can Get Better

Love enables you to put your deepest feelings and fears in the palm of your partner's hand, knowing they will be handled with care.

Carl S. Avery

If you're at a place where you think your marriage is beyond hope, this chapter is for you. It is possible to restore hope in your marriage. You can return to the place and time when you believed your partner was capable of being the husband you always thought you deserved. If you have started praising each other instead of tearing each other down, as you learned to do in the last chapter, you should already see some rays of hope.

Blaming the other person doesn't lead to change. Making excuses for your own behavior doesn't lead to change. Pretending everything is fine doesn't lead to change. True hope lies in accepting the reality of your situation, making a firm commitment not to live that way anymore, and learning how to transform your relationship in new and amazing ways.

A couple came into my office a few years ago. The wife had called to set up the appointment and had not given me much information about what was happening. I have clients fill out paperwork in the waiting room before they come in to meet with me, and neither of these folks filled in many of the responses. Their answers were very terse and didn't reveal much about what the issues were.

However, I did notice they both rated the likelihood they would stay married extremely low. Often I have one partner who rates their desire to stay married as lower than the other, but even low ratings are usually in the 3–4 range. Most couples respond with a 7 or higher, which makes sense when they are seeking marriage counseling. In this case, the husband circled a 1 and the wife a 2, making me curious as to why they were seeking marriage counseling.

When I asked them about their ratings, they revealed that they had both contacted attorneys and had planned to file for divorce. However, as they began the process of divorce proceedings, a mutual friend suggested they should at least *try* counseling before giving up completely.

As we processed this further, they both admitted they were not expecting anything positive to come out of the counseling experience. Seeing me wasn't a last-ditch effort to save the marriage. Counseling was like a box they could check so that years later they could say, "Well, we tried counseling, but it didn't work."

At this point, some counselors would decline to see the couple and suggest they save their money for the lawyers. I could have done that, but it felt like that was the easy way out. I have a reputation as a straight shooter who is not afraid of confrontation in counseling, so I decided to try the direct approach.

I told them that it didn't feel intellectually honest to come to counseling with the expectation that it would fail and that it would make more sense for the attorneys and divorce court to serve as the fail-safe plan. They could certainly call lawyers in the future if they wanted to.

I offered an alternative, asking them to commit to three months of counseling with the agreement that both would be willing to put everything on the table for negotiation: his job, her job, their possessions, their time, and even their egos. In return, I promised to help them discover what types of transformation might be possible in their marriage. I didn't promise them miraculous results (although I have seen some truly miraculous things happen in counseling). Actually, I told them they might just end up going to the lawyers anyway.

I did promise them that if they would commit to this time, effort, and flexibility, they would leave the process knowing that whether they chose to stay married or not, they had given it their best shot. I wanted them to be able to look back ten years later and know they had not thrown away the investment they had made in each other without a fight—and a good fight at that. I also told them I felt it was my professional duty to see them only if they agreed to these conditions, and that if they didn't feel this was acceptable, I would refer them to colleagues who might be able to provide other services.

This is one of those stories that has a happy ending, which is not unusual. I see far more happy endings than sad endings in my work. This counseling stuff, when it's done right, really works. This couple stuck with the process, attended three months of counseling as they had agreed to do, and then kept coming back. They began to enjoy what was happening in the relationship so much we never talked about attorneys or divorce again. Hope had taken root in the marriage.

I can't say for sure how they are doing now, as I haven't heard from them in years. One of the occupational hazards in my work is that I rarely get updates from clients to find out if things continue to go well. I do know that, after several more months of therapy, they learned to make small changes that led to larger successes. They let go of destructive beliefs they had stubbornly held on to and they developed much greater hope in the future of their marriage. Once they believed in each other again, the real work of transformation in the marriage began.

Why This Story Matters

"Fool me once, shame on you. Fool me twice, shame on me." So many partners in marriage have been hurt when they fell off the horse (or the snowboard or bicycle, whatever analogy works for you). Everyone tells them they need to get back up and try again, but it seems foolish to do something again that was so painful the first time. So why does anyone try to get back up and ride? The pure joy and satisfaction they feel when they do get back up drives them to do it again.

It may have been a long time since you experienced that joy in your marriage, and you may not even remember what it feels like. That's the reason you feel that the love is gone and the spark has died. You can't have hope in the future of love if you can't remember how it felt or don't see any way you can get it back. The thing about being in love, though, is that if you did it once, you can do it again. Contrary to public opinion, love didn't just happen *to* you. You were a big part of creating the love that developed.

How many times in the past year have you talked about your hopes and dreams for the future together? Most of the conversations have been arguments or problem solving, right? If after those difficult discussions you don't have a soft place to land, created by positive, fun, enjoyable times together, then it seems that all there is to the marriage is anger, resentment, frustration, and disappointment. There's no room for hope in a relationship like that.

Hope is vitally important for a controlling husband. Remember, a huge reason men become controlling is their fear of being out of control and their feelings of insecurity. If they can come to believe that there is another way, they will consider following that path, as most controlling husbands do not actually enjoy the pain and frustration they cause those around them. For these men, hope involves believing that there is a way to feel safe, secure, and loved without controlling their wives. This process starts with seeing success in small, less risky situations.

Hope Starts with Small Successes

One of the first steps in restoring hope to a marriage is to identify some small, but achievable, goals. Suppose you are a wife who has had great difficulty communicating in your marriage. This could be because you are afraid of upsetting your husband with the truth or he is too prideful to ask for help. Maybe you both quit trying to talk to each other about things other than the kids and work years ago and have settled into a routine that doesn't require any meaningful communication.

You could spend months or even years trying to overhaul your communication skills. However, you will likely give up long before you achieve that lofty goal. A better approach would be to choose the number one communication problem that is causing difficulty in your daily life right now. Develop a plan to make a small change, starting today, in that one area. Once you see the positive effect this small change has, point it out to your partner so he or she can try it. Then hold each other accountable to make progress each day in that one area. You don't have to solve the problem in a day. You just have to make specific, measureable changes that will lead to your both feeling a sense of achievement and of moving the relationship in the right direction.

For instance, you might be having trouble finding time to communicate. A small, measurable change would be to set aside ten minutes each day that both of you protect as sacred time during which you can bring up issues that either of you are concerned about. You may not have anything important to talk about during that time, but just learning to make that time available is a success you can both celebrate.

Hope in Our Marriage

Much of the difficulty I have created in my life is due to my own negativity. My fear of the unknown has prevented me from living life to the fullest. It has certainly affected my marriage. However, in recent years, as I have worked hard to change this part of me and to transform myself as a husband and as a father, an interesting development has taken place in our marriage. I knew I was selfish, overreactive, angry, and difficult to live with. As I worked to change these aspects of my personality, I discovered that everything that goes wrong in the marriage is not my fault. That may not seem like a big revelation to you. However, when you are trying to get a husband who has been a controller and manipulator for much of his life to consider changing, this is a big deal. It helps to know that power and control in your marriage involve both partners. Jan and I have become brutally honest in these areas. We tell each other exactly what we think and feel, rather than letting resentment boil under the surface and cause damage over time.

If you are a controlling husband who is considering the process of transformation, knowing that the problems are not 100 percent your fault can give you a great deal of hope. One of the great myths about controlling husbands is that they are truly despicable people who enjoy hurting others. The truth is that most controlling husbands would jump at the chance to get their needs met without hurting their wives if they could see another way to feel safe and secure. They just don't see any other options. When they begin to see that their partner can help them change by holding them accountable and changing what they do to encourage controlling behavior, they don't feel solely responsible.

Rather than serving as accountability partners for each other, I recommend that you both develop at least one or two solid accountability partners outside of the marriage. These individuals should be older, the same sex as you, and have learned to overcome challenges similar to those you are facing in your marriage. Tell them the areas of your behavior you want to change in the marriage and ask them to hold you accountable by meeting with you at least every other week to talk about how you are doing.

The Changes That Are Needed

I am extremely encouraged and hopeful about the changes Jan is making in her life. Like me, she is having to change for her own benefit as well as for our relationship. Her anger and bitterness toward me were holding her back from her own development. She began to assume that all our problems were my fault and resented any suggestion that there were areas she needed to change.

It took Jan a couple of years to believe that I was capable of changing my controlling behavior and even longer to believe I could maintain the changes. Even today, she catches herself expecting me to respond in a controlling manner in a certain situation and realizes she has no reason to do so. She has told me that part of the challenge she faced, and that you may face also, is getting past the bitterness and anger she felt about the way I had treated her.

One of the things that helped her overcome this was letting go of the power she actually gained by holding on to that resentment. In a strange way, holding my previous controlling behavior against me gave her more power in the relationship because I kept having to make up for the mistakes I had made in the past. The power actually shifted the opposite way, leaving the relationship unbalanced again. When she began to truly forgive me, our relationship became more stable and she found the ability to expect me to succeed in becoming the husband she hoped I could be.

She also found that as I became less intimidating, it was easier to talk to me about her feelings. This still remains hard for her, but telling me how she feels helps her put her resentment and anger behind. Each time she experiences me listening to her and trying to understand her, the previous images of an unreasonable, controlling husband become less powerful. She can begin to respond to me as the man I am rather than the man I was.

I mention this because I believe that this road to transformation is a two-lane highway that both partners need to travel together. Each of you will need to change and grow. Hope in your marriage will develop as you both see each other trying to think of the other first, honoring the other, and respecting the other.

Hope Exercise 1: Have Fun!

One of the exercises that I give couples who are struggling with hope may not seem like rocket science. I ask them to find an activity they both enjoy and—wait for it—go have fun! What a concept, right? Look, when is the last time you truly enjoyed being together? I don't mean just watching a movie or eating dinner. You can do that with anyone.

I'm talking about doing something as a couple when you can enjoy being in each other's company and talking to each other. Think of hobbies or activities that you have in common or come up with something new. Choose an activity and schedule time to have fun together. You cannot rebuild your marriage by discussing problems all the time. You need to balance this with enjoying each other's company.

Hope Exercise 2: Remember When

Remembering when things in the relationship weren't as bad as they seem to be now can help create hope. When was the last time you had the type of fun I talked about in exercise 1? For some couples, the last time they remember having fun was during their honeymoon; some even have to think back to when they were engaged.

For most couples, though, there were times, perhaps early in the marriage, when they really enjoyed being together. What about you? Maybe it was before you had kids or perhaps it was back when the pressure of your careers wasn't so overwhelming. It might have been when there was an innocence to your relationship and it felt like the two of you could overcome anything that life threw at you.

Take some time to remember when things were better between you. Talk with each other about how and why you fell in love. If you experienced beauty in your relationship for a season, you can feel that way again. You know how to do it because you've done it before. You just have to remember the conditions that were in place, the ways that you treated each other, and the priorities you had that made *that* relationship possible. There is great hope in the knowledge that you already know what to do; you just have to make the changes necessary to do what you have done before.

Hope Exercise 3: Identify Strengths

During an evening when you and your partner are calm, relaxed, and not frustrated with each other, choose a location where you are both comfortable talking. Together, write down everything that either of you can come up with that you do well in your marriage.

The goal of this exercise is to name out loud every strength that you have as a couple. Make sure you write down small and large strengths. Examples could be that you have similar interests, handle money well, or laugh at the same jokes. Perhaps you deal with crises well as a team, or work together well as parents. When you are done, you should have a solid list of the strengths in your marriage that you can use to build hope and confidence for the future.

More Hope Exercises

There is an outstanding resource available for you to use for rebuilding hope in your marriage. Everett Worthington has written a wonderful book, *Hope-Focused Marriage Counseling*,[1] in which he offers exercises for building hope back into your marriage in a variety of different areas. If you would like some additional practice in this area, I highly recommend his book to you.

Moving Forward

Believing in each other is the key to rebuilding hope in your marriage. You may have forgotten how much more effective you can be as a team than you are apart. You may have even let yourself believe your spouse is holding you back. Injecting hope back into your ailing relationship can be just what the doctor ordered. It gives you the strength to move forward to the next steps in transformation.

16

Forgiving Each Other

Leaving the Past Behind

Love is an act of endless forgiveness, a tender look which becomes a habit.

Peter Ustinov

I'm sorry. These two words may seem so incredibly easy to say, yet do these two words do any good if they don't seem sincere or aren't backed up by actions? Divorces have occurred over a lack of forgiveness. Bitterness and resentment can build up and last a lifetime. Two people who stood in front of God and their family and friends and professed undying love for each other can become filled with spite and hate.

What do you do with all that frustration and anger? I've heard so many reasons not to forgive. "He has told me time and time again that he would change. Why on earth should I trust him again?" "Fool me once . . ." The worst part is, he knows how hard it is for you to trust that he will change and then he goes and hurts you all over again. When is it enough? Why should you forgive him again?

What you need to understand is that for your husband to change, you have to believe he can change and expect him to change. By this point in the transformation process, both partners have begun to praise each other more, noticing and rewarding the positive, supportive things they do for each other. This change has led to renewed hope that the relationship can change and doesn't have to be the way it has been.

Unfortunately, I have worked with many couples who made it this far, and then the relationship is torpedoed by a lack of forgiveness. Bitterness and resentment over past mistakes overwhelms the praise and hope that had begun to form. Husbands who have begun to consider really changing their behavior lose all their momentum when wives continue to expect them to fail. He won't succeed every time—it may even be two steps forward and one step back. You certainly will need to maintain the boundaries we have discussed and set clear, measurable expectations. But you must allow him the opportunity to become the man you hope he can be and not keep him a prisoner of your anger, resentment, and regret over the past.

Bitterness and Resentment

Holding bitterness and resentment inside is a recipe for disaster. The things that upset you about your spouse or your relationship won't go away. In fact they tend to build on each other, with one unresolved conflict setting the stage for a larger conflict the next time. However, The Stanford Forgiveness Project[1] showed that people who forgive, instead of holding bitterness and resentment inside, showed significant decreases in emotional pain, long-term anger, and physical symptoms of stress. Even more important, Frank Fincham and his fellow researchers found that when wives forgave their husbands, the couples were better able to resolve conflicts a year later. Letting the resentment go really does help.[2]

Think of it this way—if you get a splinter in your finger and you either can't or won't take it out (perhaps because of the pain that it will involve), you can just put a Band-Aid over it and hope it goes away. Most often, however, it doesn't get better, an infection sets in, and it gets worse. That's how it is with conflict. If you don't bring it out in the open and deal with it, it festers inside. Just like an infected finger can result in gangrene and the amputation of a limb, untreated emotional wounds lead to bitterness and resentment that can turn a kind, loving person into a spiteful, angry individual.

What Forgiveness Is Not

Forgiving but Not Forgetting

You've heard people say, "I will forgive but I won't forget." I understand why people say it but I don't agree with the underlying premise. If you want to forgive someone, why would you be committed to remembering the anger and bitterness and resentment you feel? I think it is because at some level you don't want to forgive the person—at least not completely. You want to do the right thing and you care about what others think of you and want to maintain the image of a forgiving person, but you don't want to forget what has been done to you.

It's difficult not to hold someone's previous behavior against them. If you let go of something that someone has done to you, you may be risking more hurt in the future. To minimize being taken advantage of again, you should say the right things but maintain a clear distrust of the person.

Here's the problem: if you can't trust someone or if you expect less of her or him based on previous behavior, then I question whether you have really forgiven the person. I'm not suggesting that humans are capable of wiping their memories clean (other than on one of those corny Syfy Channel movies). I am suggesting that if you truly forgive someone, you will treat them as if what they did never happened. I mentioned in the last chapter that Jan had to learn to forgive me in order to stop expecting me to control her. You will have to forgive your husband or you will continue to expect him to fail.

Withholding Trust

I worked with a couple many years ago who could each cite chapter and verse of incidents that had occurred between the two of them ten, fifteen, even twenty years before. They almost never had a discussion that didn't involve comments like, "That doesn't make up for what you did at Christmas back in 1982 . . ." or "Okay, but that's nothing compared to how bad you were on our vacation in '76." Every current relationship experience was seen in light of previous behavior.

It took us the better part of a year to work through this issue. They were both scared of letting go of the past. Being able to recall the times when each had been hurt in the past represented control and power over their spouse. They didn't want to give up that power and become vulnerable again.

True forgiveness should lead to increased trust. If you find yourself expecting that your spouse is going to let you down, forgiveness is probably not happening.

Expecting Failure

Expecting the one you love to fail is another warning sign that forgiveness may be absent in your marriage. If you are able to forgive your spouse and let the past go, it follows that you would not be pessimistic about your relationship. In other words, truly forgiving your spouse would lead to an expectation of success and a great deal of hope for the future of your relationship.

In the absence of forgiveness, the relationship is shrouded in a dark cloud of despair where there is an expectation of failure. Strong memories of previous disappointments lead to certainty that your spouse, who has let you down before, will do so again.

When we make assumptions based on our experiences, it is difficult to change them. This can be seen when we walk into a room and immediately make assumptions based on what people look like, how they are dressed, and what color their skin is. We are quick to look for confirmation of what we already believe. Psychologist Peter Wason coined a phrase for this: *confirmation bias*.[3] It basically means that when you believe something is true, you expect to find evidence to support what you already believe and tend to dismiss things that would convince you otherwise. We like to think we are right and we look for evidence to prove we are right.

This has implications when there is a need for forgiveness. It takes two people to make forgiveness happen. Your partner may apologize, you may believe the apology is sincere, and his behavior may even get better after the apology, but you still have a part to play. As long as you keep assuming your spouse is going to screw up and is still the person he has always been, forgiveness hasn't happened, at least not completely.

If you continue to expect your partner to fail, you won't notice if they succeed. For instance, you may have come to believe that your husband will always correct what you say. You start assuming that this is simply a character trait: *it's just who he is*. How can he be expected to change, or even want to, when the person who supposedly loves him the most has given up on the possibility that he can change? You end up paying attention to the one time he corrects you and ignore the ten times he doesn't. I continue to be amazed at the creative ability couples have to sabotage change in a relationship, even when they both agree the change would be good. Often the driving force in this resistance to change is a lack of forgiveness.

The problem with expecting failure is that people have this annoying habit of behaving in the ways you expect them to behave. Psychologist Robert Merton called this a *self-fulfilling prophecy*.[4] As long as you continue to hold on to the things that have gone wrong in the relationship, you will define your spouse in that way and expect him or her to fail in the future. And as long as you expect your partner to fail, he or she will be happy to do so.

Keeping Your Distance

Another indicator of the absence of forgiveness is the presence of distance and disconnection in the relationship. It's the reason one partner asks the other, "Are we okay?" This question is an effort to find out if the relationship is back to *normal* and the earthquake they just experienced is over, or if there are going to be ongoing aftershocks that will have to be weathered. Keep in mind that even an affirmative "Yeah, we're okay," may not mean things are fine. It may just be that the person being asked doesn't want to deal with the consequences of answering, "No, we are not okay."

Regardless of how the question is answered, there are numerous indicators that provide a clear measurement of the relationship status without having to look it up on Facebook. People find ways to keep a safe distance from their partner when they don't feel ready to reengage. Finding reasons to be out of the house or away from the other person, not talking about anything other than extremely superficial issues, and giving brief, terse responses to questions are all indications that things are not back to *normal*. You can probably identify the specific indicators in your relationship.

For Jan and me, these types of status indicators are quite different. I know that she is still upset with me if she stays busy doing other things, goes out of her way to say "I'm fine" and won't look me in the eyes, or changes the subject whenever I ask about the thing we were disagreeing about. Jan tells me that when I am too quiet, get upset over small things, or respond with short, terse comments, she knows something is wrong. Despite our best efforts, we are rarely able to hide our frustration, disappointment, or anger from each other. After twenty-seven years of marriage, we both know what it feels like when we are okay and when we are not.

What Forgiveness Is

Perhaps the most difficult part of forgiveness is moving forward as if the incident that you need to forgive never happened. Letting go of this perceived wrong requires several things. First, you have to let go of the need for justice, as forgiveness has nothing to do with justice. Second, you have to let go of the need to hold on to power over the other person because forgiveness involves letting go of control in the situation. Finally, you have to let go of the need for security; if justice and power are sacrificed, you will be left feeling very vulnerable and unsafe.

Relinquishing Justice

There are no two ways about it—forgiving someone is not fair. There is no justice or equality in it. If you are going to forgive, you are engaging in a process that is unfair by definition. Someone offended you, and in your soul, you think he or she should pay a price. However, your assumption that this is a zero-sum game is a faulty premise. When you forgive, you have to give up the idea that there must be a winner and a loser.

When Clint Eastwood stares down the bad guy in the *Dirty Harry* movie and says, "Go ahead—make my day," we know we should hope the bad guy lays down his gun and goes peacefully. However, another part of us thinks he deserves what's coming to him and hopes Clint makes him pay.

A politician says something offensive; justice says his or her political career should be over. A husband cheats on his wife; justice says he deserves what he gets when she divorces him, as the betrayal must be punished. This is the world we live in; it is not forgiving. Justice is a far stronger driving force in our world than forgiveness.

If you need further evidence of this, just look at how quick the media is to find someone or something to blame for everything that makes news. Before the facts are in, news outlets make accusations and assumptions with little or no evidence. We cannot stand to have something happen without assigning responsibility. If it isn't clear who is at fault, we'll make an accusation anyway, whether or not it has any basis in fact.

In *The Complete Marriage Book*, Tim and Julie Clinton state, "Forgiveness is always *my* responsibility, even as I have been wronged. It means canceling a debt. That's something I do within myself." They go on to say, "When I choose to forgive, it frees me to love."[5]

True forgiveness, then, means giving up our seemingly innate desire to have our relationships be fair and for people to pay the price they should pay. In fact forgiving our spouse means looking them straight in the eye, knowing they are at fault for what happened, and choosing not to hold them accountable. This is completely countercultural in a world that demands justice for everything. Then again, doesn't doing the right thing often go against what the world around us would have us do?

For the wife of a controlling husband this is very difficult to do. Even if you agree with me that forgiveness is better than holding a grudge (at least in terms of a healthy relationship), it feels like he is getting off easy. *If I always forgive him, what reason will he have to change?* The danger in this thought process is that you assume that maintaining resentment and not forgiving him will somehow force him to change. In reality this almost never works. Be honest—how often has it worked for you?

Not forgiving your husband helps you maintain power and control—it's as if he owes you because of his previous failures. This may feel good, but it is *not* a healthy relationship pattern. The power may shift, but it's a shift based on revenge and resentment, and it just contributes to that you vs. him mentality I've mentioned before. Forgiveness breeds trust, trust breeds intimacy, and intimacy breeds love. I know it's a difficult choice, but I believe it's worth the risk.

Giving Away Power

When you forgive, you are absolutely giving away power. You cannot forgive and maintain the same level of power and control you will have if you do not forgive. I have thought about this a lot recently in terms of how my wife and I forgive each other.

Often I say things I regret later, so I have had to work hard to watch what I say and how it affects Jan. She feels things deeply and can be easily hurt in ways that take a long time for her to get over.

As Jan has been the less powerful person in our relationship, it makes all the sense in the world for her to hold on to the power that not forgiving provides. The power imbalance that is created when one partner offends the other is alleviated by forgiveness. The partner who was wronged may not want to give back that power after the offense has occurred. I am now much more aware of the sacrifice Jan has to make to forgive me, as she has a lot more to lose by forgiving than I realized.

Letting Go of Security

Forgiveness creates a feeling of vulnerability. Our language is replete with adages that illustrate the risk we take when we trust someone who has wronged us—getting back on the horse; fool me once, shame on you; fool me twice, shame on me; out of the frying pan and into the fire. We are all too familiar with the unsettling feeling that forgiveness creates.

However, it doesn't have to be this way. This is not a fear of the unknown. Actually the future is more known to us *after* we have been hurt than it was before. The betrayal has already occurred and we know how much it hurts. The question now is, do we want to risk getting hurt and feeling that way again or choose the safer route and remain resentful?

Forgiving someone is an act of courage. It is standing up and saying to the world, and to the person who wronged you, *I love you enough to give you a second chance*. In a world that rarely offers them, second chances are what forgiveness is all about. That makes the experience all the more powerful and meaningful when it occurs.

I am not diminishing the risk and vulnerability that forgiveness entails. Your spouse may hurt you again. However, we are not talking about trusting Joe Schmo off the street. This is the person you have chosen to spend your life with. If you can't trust the person you are married to, whom can you trust? I know he has given you reason not to trust him in the past. If he is changing now, though, you need to respond based on his current behavior. This may be a weekly or even daily choice that you have to make.

Perhaps you are asking the wrong question when it comes to forgiveness and security. Over the life of your marriage, how many times have you trusted this person with your true self, with your soul, with your heart? Rather than counting the times you have been betrayed or let down, perhaps you should consider counting the times he or she *has* been there for you. Your partner's batting average may be higher than you think.

The Importance of Repentance

Forgiveness is one of the central tenets of the Christian faith. Born out of the belief that human beings are sinful creatures who need forgiveness, this idea forms the core of the need for the sacrifice of Jesus on the cross. I believe that Christ's example is relevant and useful for all of us to look at as a model of what forgiveness can look like.

Craig Blomberg suggests that forgiveness does not involve enabling controlling individuals' behavior.[6] Noting the oft-quoted Matthew 18:21–22, Blomberg discusses Jesus's response to Peter's question, "Lord, how many times shall I forgive my brother or sister who sins against me? Up to seven times?" Jesus answered, "I tell you, not seven times, but seventy-seven times."

Blomberg believes that Jesus was probably referring to a larger number to indicate that forgiveness should not have limitations. Indeed, the King James wording of "seventy times seven" depicts an even larger number. Blomberg further clarifies that the surrounding passages provide a context for forgiveness that helps us understand what genuine repentance looks like, as well as the expectation that the forgiven person repent and make substantial efforts to change his or her behavior.

In your marriage relationship, what makes you believe that the person you love has actually *repented* or *really means it* when he says, "I'm sorry"? How do you know if someone is sincere in her apology? Some people say it's the look on her face or the tears in his eyes. Most people seem to report that nonverbal factors convince them more than words.

It really does take two to dance the tango of forgiveness. You need to let go of the need for justice, release the power that holding on to resentment creates, and allow yourself to feel vulnerable again. Your partner needs to repent and give you a reason to trust again. When you both make this commitment to forgiveness and repentance, your relationship can be transformed in truly beautiful ways.

17

Serving Each Other

Learning to Think of the Other First

Love comes when manipulation stops; when you think more about the other person than about his or her reactions to you.

Dr. Joyce Brothers

You don't need to be on Facebook to know that relationships are *complicated*. Each time I think I have heard every variation on a potential theme, something new comes up. It's one of the things that makes being a psychologist so interesting.

Just once, I'd love for someone to walk in to my office and say, "You know what, Doc? This is all my fault. If I could only become a better person and change what I'm doing, the marriage would be so much better." Instead, what I usually hear is, "If he would only . . ." or "If she would only . . ."

Usually couples come to therapy making the case for what the other person needs to change if the relationship is to improve. Tim Keller, in *The Meaning of Marriage*, says that "self-centeredness is a havoc wreaking problem in many marriages, and it is the ever-present enemy of *every* marriage."[1] He believes that husbands and wives must be willing to see their own selfishness as the fundamental problem if they want to change their relationship.

The following quiz will show you what your priorities are. You can take it with your husband.

The Marriage Priority Quiz

For each of the following statements, which is more important to you:

_____ Proving your point OR _____ Building up your spouse's confidence

_____ Winning the argument OR _____ Letting your spouse win

_____ Feeling good about yourself OR _____ Your spouse feeling good about him- or herself

_____ Getting your way OR _____ Resolving the issue

_____ Being proud of yourself OR _____ Being proud of your spouse

_____ Making the decision your way OR _____ Growing closer together as a couple

If you marked any of the items in the left column, you should be concerned. If you marked several of them, your level of selfishness may be significantly affecting your marriage.

Selflessness and Controlling Husbands

Here's a quick test for husbands to determine what they actually believe about the issue of selflessness. If your husband isn't reading this book, you can give him the test. I call it The Super Bowl Test. If the man in the relationship is not a football fan, you can substitute whatever event is the highlight of his year (another sports event, the yearly fishing trip, the Star Trek convention, or whatever his thing is).

The Super Bowl Test for Husbands

You are excited about the upcoming Super Bowl and have invited several friends over to watch the big game. You and the guys have been talking about it for weeks and this is a big deal for you.

An hour or so before the big game starts, your wife receives a call from her mother. Her mom smells something strange in her house. Your wife is worried it might be gas and wants you to go over with her and see if everything is okay. Her mom lives more than an hour away, and you know you will miss at least part of the game, if not all of it. Your wife says her mom doesn't know how to tell if the smell is dangerous or not. She tells you that she knows her mom might be overreacting, but she is afraid there may be a real danger.

You have several choices here. Do you:

1. Call the gas company or 911 and tell your wife they will take care of it?
2. Tell your wife to drive to her mom's house without you?
3. Take your wife to your mom's house, miss the game, and make sure your wife knows how unhappy you are?
4. Take your wife to your mom's house, miss the game, and have a positive attitude the entire time?

You see, this is where the rubber meets the road. Choices have consequences. This is definitely a pass/fail test, and you can bet you will be spending some time in detention if you mess this up. It may seem like you are being put in an unfair position; after all, it's the Super Bowl! But if you put your wife first only when it's convenient for you, you're not making her needs a priority. The times when you are the most tired and pressured may be the times when she most needs you to show her that you can put her needs before your own.

If I have to choose between a relationship where both parties are fighting to get their needs met or one in which each partner is working as hard as possible to meet the other's needs, I will always choose the latter. The reality of limited resources will always lead to conflict in the first scenario, and that can often become a lose-lose experience. I believe the alternative approach is much more of a win-win option, capitalizing on all the available resources in the relationship. It requires trust because both parties have to believe the other has their best interests at heart, but the latter option can lead to a much more fulfilling marriage.

Models of Marriage

When is the last time you saw a television ad or an Internet website that showed marriage partners sacrificing for each other? The media promotes looking out for number one. We are constantly told that relationships are about what you can get out of them, and that people who are intelligent and insightful leave relationships that don't make them happy or meet their needs. Marriage is portrayed more as an extended sexual hookup than a lifelong commitment—get your needs met, stay as long as you are happy, and leave when your needs are not being met.

Despite all our mistakes, Jan and I have always held a different view of marriage. We believe that marriage is a lifelong commitment, so when we have encountered storms in our marriage, the "D" word was never on the table. We've never considered giving up on the relationship because we wanted something different; we have focused our efforts on becoming the best partners we can be.

In the Christian faith tradition, there is a concept known as *servanthood*. It's based on the example Jesus set of putting others' needs first and sacrificing himself for others. Christian husbands are told specifically in Paul's letter to the Ephesians to be willing to sacrifice their own lives for their wives. This idea of serving the other person above your own needs has significant relevance for marriage today, as it is a stark contrast to the "me first" mentality seen in the prevailing models of marriage.

You hear the terms *selflessness* and *sacrifice* used interchangeably at times. Looking at these words more closely, one learns that there is a subtle difference in their meaning. Being *selfless* is defined by Webster as "having no concern for self," while *sacrifice* is defined as "something given up or lost." The concept of servanthood in marriage includes both: focusing on your partner rather than yourself *and* giving up some of what you want or need for her or him.

I have always loved C. S. Lewis—his words speak to me on so many levels. I recently read again his chapter on Christian marriage in *Mere Christianity*. In that chapter Lewis argues for a model of marriage that involves commitment to a partner even after the honeymoon phase wears off. Lewis says, "In fact, whatever people say, the state called 'being in love' usually does not last. If the old fairy-tale ending 'They lived happily ever after' is taken to mean 'They felt for the next fifty years exactly as they felt the day before they were married,' then it says what probably never was nor ever could be true. . . . In this department of life, as in every other, thrills come at the beginning and do not last." He continues: "People get from books the idea that if you have married the right person you may expect to go on 'being in love' forever. As a result, when they find they are not, they think this proves they have made a mistake and are entitled to a change."[2]

A marriage in which both partners focus on the needs of the other allows the freedom for partners to grow and change. Lewis speaks to this point, as well. "It is just the people who are ready to submit to the loss of the thrill and settle down to the sober interest, who are then most likely to meet new thrills in some quite different direction. The man who has learned to fly and becomes a good pilot will suddenly discover music." He goes on to say, "This is, I think, one little part of what Christ meant by saying that a good thing will not really live unless it first dies. It is simply no good trying to keep any thrill: that is the very worst thing you can do. Let the thrill go—let it die away . . . and you will find you are living in a world of new thrills all the time."[3]

Selfishness and Unspoken Rules

In any relationship, I believe there are "unspoken rules." An unspoken rule is a behavior practiced by one or both of you that neither partner questions. It is just tacitly accepted as "the way we do it." I talk at length to couples about this. For instance, it may be an accepted fact that Steve is going to watch sports on Sunday afternoon. It isn't up for negotiation, as Diane accepts that they will come home after church, eat a meal, and she won't hear much from Steve for the rest of the day. In this same marriage, Steve and Diane may both agree not to talk about her previous relationship, for she has made it clear that the issue is not open for discussion. Steve may have stopped asking about it years ago, tacitly agreeing to the unspoken rule.

These unspoken rules provide immense insight into the challenges that exist in a relationship. However, the rules usually involve sensitive issues and can create significant conflict in the relationship if they are questioned. Often therapists who work with couples report hitting a nerve that they didn't know existed. It's like when a construction crew is digging in a yard, and the gas or electric company has not marked the lines correctly. The crew knows instantly when they have hit a line they didn't know existed, as the consequences are severe and immediate.

These unspoken rules are very important to understanding controlling husbands. Controlling behavior reinforces itself, and soon both partners simply accept that she does what he wants. That unspoken rule has to change. To replace this old rule with a new one, the controlling husband must consider one of the most difficult changes he has to make. I will not suggest that this is an easy step in the process—on the contrary, your husband may resist this part of the process more than any other.

It is at this point that he has to decide if he is going to choose to commit to you and to your marriage. There is a point at which he must make this choice. It is really quite similar to the decision he made when he proposed to you and when he said, "I do." I have worked with couples who have chosen to take this so seriously that they made the decision to renew their vows at this point. In fact, I highly recommend considering a formal ceremony to renew your vows at the point when you both have decided to recommit to the marriage. It can be an extremely powerful way of marking the beginning of a new season in your relationship.

I worked with a couple once whose unspoken rules were very clear. Denise and Lance had a huge number of these rules that they described as "just the way it is" in their relationship. For instance, Lance had a temper, and despite her frustration with his anger, Denise just accepted that if she pushed him too hard on something, he would blow up. He would stay mad just a little while and he would always apologize, and that was just the way things were.

Other unspoken rules in their relationship included the following:

- Lance was more intelligent than Denise (FYI—I didn't give them IQ tests, but my money was on Denise as the brighter one).
- Lance could play sports any time he wanted, and Denise was expected to watch the kids. However, Denise would have to schedule time if she wanted Lance to watch the kids while she went out with her friends.
- Denise did the housework and took care of the kids—period.
- Lance provided the income (Denise didn't work outside of the home) and he did the yard work. Any additional requests for help with the house and kids were unacceptable.
- Denise could trump everything by crying and becoming depressed. Lance would worry about Denise hurting herself (she had engaged in self-harm behaviors in the past), so by crying and becoming depressed, Denise could manipulate Lance into doing what she wanted.

Unspoken Rules Exercise

This is an exercise that you can ask your husband to do with you even if he is not committed to significant change. It can help you identify the unspoken rules in your marriage.

1. You and your spouse will each write down ten statements that you believe are unspoken rules that you both have accepted in your marriage. Make each statement as clear and precise as possible, so it represents exactly what you believe is true about your relationship.

2. After both of you have created your separate lists, sit down together to compare lists.

   - Highlight the rules that appear on both lists; these have been accepted as "truth" by both of you.
   - Discuss the rules that one listed and the other did not, and decide if you both want to agree with these rules.
   - Discuss which rules you may both agree should be discarded because they are not effective.
   - Discuss which rules need to be adapted in order to be effective.

Unspoken Rules, Power, and Serving Each Other in Marriage

The reason these unspoken truths are so important in marriage is that these are the issues where power/control and the opposite, service/servanthood, are most relevant. These are the important issues, the ones that are most central to the relationship. If you can stop enforcing these rules and instead learn to serve each other in these areas, then putting the toilet seat down will be a breeze, compared to other acts of service you do.

Think of what an impact it would have on Denise if Lance stopped assuming she would take care of the kids whenever he wanted to be gone. How much more would Lance respect and honor Denise if she stopped using emotional and mental health issues to manipulate him? Once you identify these unspoken rules in your marriage, they can become a guide for how you can serve each other.

Serving Each Other—the Marital Vision

One of the best ways to develop an atmosphere of selflessness and sacrifice in your marriage is to develop a clear and well-thought-out vision for your marriage. In truth, this should be part of every couple's premarital counseling, but it rarely is. Too often premarital counseling focuses on communication skills or wedding plans rather than the deeper, more transformational issues of character development and vision planning. This is the reason I ask couples who see me for premarital work to continue to see me after the wedding, when reality sets in and they see the people they actually married.

Creating a marital vision involves being honest with each other and talking about your hopes and dreams for the future. This can be an incredible time of bonding. Each person can share what they truly want out of life and what the future would be like if they could have their wishes. Couples can get caught up in the daily routine and discover that their lives are running them, rather than the other way around.

Developing a marital vision involves understanding how you and your spouse are a *gestalt*: the whole is greater than the sum of its parts. What is unique and special about the two of you together? What skills and abilities do you possess as a team that you wouldn't have alone? Each partner can strengthen the other; in my faith tradition we call this "iron sharpening iron" (see Prov. 27:17).

The unique qualities you have as a couple create the cornerstones of a marital vision. You develop a plan for the future that will maximize the strengths that each of you brings to the table, and this leads to a vision of what unique and creative things you can do as a couple. It is important that both of you share honestly your hopes and dreams for the future.

As your relationship matures and is transformed, you will begin to see the value of dedicating yourself to helping your partner's dreams come true, even more than your own. When you experience the joy of putting the needs of your partner above your own, and see the joy he or she feels in doing the same for you, the beauty of this type of relationship becomes clear. As you serve each other, instead of focusing on yourself, you will experience a depth of intimacy in the relationship that you never felt before. I am confident that it will leave you wanting to serve each other in even more creative and sacrificial ways.

Part Six

Making It
All Work

18

Seeking Professional Help

I've experienced several different healing methodologies over the years—counseling, self-help seminars, and I've read a lot—but none of them will work unless you really want to heal.

Lindsay Wagner

One of the best steps you can take to begin to transform your relationship is to engage in marriage counseling. Some of the steps you have learned in this book you may accomplish on your own. However, there are changes that may require the help of a marriage counselor. You may need the counselor to encourage your husband to make some of the changes you are hoping for, while other steps may simply be more complex than you expected. In any case, there are things marriage counseling can do and other things it cannot do.

All marriage counseling is not equal. Some of you may have had wonderful experiences in counseling, and I rejoice with you at those successes. Others of you may have tried marriage counseling without any success. When you multiply the numerous types of therapy by the individual differences of each therapist, there are as many types of marital therapy as there are marriages.

Even if your husband agreed to go, there is no guarantee that a specific counselor in a specific setting will be a good match for helping him understand the changes that are needed. Much of what you have learned in this book can be immediately applied in your marriage without professional help. However, it may be very difficult for you to make sustained progress without the assistance of a licensed therapist.

Making a Good Choice

Baskin-Robbins has nothing on the counseling profession. You can pretty much find any flavor, size, shape, or color of marriage counseling you are looking for. On top of that, each counselor is different and applies theories and techniques differently, and each relationship each counselor has with a couple is unique. However, some of the most effective current approaches to marital counseling focus on understanding attachments from childhood that are acted out in marriage, learning communication skills, and understanding how to separate from families of origin. Seeing one marriage counselor, or even two or three, does not mean that you have experienced the powerful transformation that is possible through counseling. There are other factors that may mean the counseling process is not successful: the match with a specific counselor may not be good, the counselor's skills may not be that great, and/or your commitment to the process may be lacking. There are a hundred different reasons why marriage counseling might not be effective in a certain situation.

When a couple calls to ask about marriage counseling, I encourage them to interview two or three other therapists. I want them to see the variety of options out there and make an informed choice about who they feel will best meet their needs and desires for counseling. If they are a faith-based couple, I encourage them to pray about the decision and seek God's guidance in the selection of a counselor, just as they would pray about any other major decision in their lives. I also tell couples who choose to meet with me to reevaluate their choice after the first couple of sessions and consider whether their experience is living up to what they had hoped for. I want them to be "all in" with the person they are going to work with.

There are those that say counseling success is entirely up to the client and it's not about the counselor. I don't agree with that. The clients do the majority of the work and they are the ones who have to change their lives and transform their marriage, but saying the counselor isn't important is like saying anyone can do brain surgery. Education, training, supervision, experience—these things all matter. The match between you and the counselor is *very* important.

So what does it take to make a successful marriage counseling relationship? It's like the old joke about how many psychologists it takes to change a lightbulb. Do you know the answer? It takes only one, but the lightbulb really has to want to change. Okay, so I won't ever be a stand-up comedian!

The point is that if you or your spouse doesn't truly *want* to change, no counselor in the world can make either of you do so. For any counseling process to work, the people involved have to have a *true desire to be transformed.*

The Reluctant Husband

If your spouse is hesitant to see a marriage counselor, there may be good reasons he feels this way. Perhaps he doesn't want to go because he is afraid you and the counselor will gang up on him and it will be "two against one." It could also be that he doesn't like others knowing your business or that he feels only "weak" people go to counseling. It is crucial to understand why he is resistant.

I have learned some successful strategies for tactfully discussing issues that are difficult to bring up with your spouse. These work extremely well when you need to talk with a spouse who is resistant to coming in for counseling. These ideas may help you discuss the idea of marriage counseling with your partner.

First, choose the time for such a conversation carefully. If there is a time pressure of any sort or he is already in a bad mood for some reason, it's not a good time to bring up the topic. You probably already know that, as I assume you have become fairly skilled at gauging his moods to avoid his anger. Find a time when you know the chances of his being positive and receptive are the best.

Second, don't present the idea of counseling as a punishment. If it consistently comes up when you are arguing, it can be perceived as an attack. If you take the role of a parent disciplining her child, it is not likely to go well. Spouses have significantly greater success discussing issues like this when they treat each other as equals, instead of trying to force each other to agree.

Third, I mentioned using "qualifiers" in chapter 14, and they are useful here. Qualifiers are statements that put the other partner at ease and prevent the situation from being confrontational or antagonistic. For instance, you could say, "I know that you feel counseling is not going to be helpful, and I'm not trying to start an argument. I just want to try to understand why you think it won't work." Or you could start the conversation by saying, "I could be completely wrong about this. I am not saying this is the right thing to do, because I really don't know for sure. I'd just like to hear your opinion." When you do this, you are asking for his help as your teammate, rather than presenting yourself as the opposition. Just as cornering a wild animal and trying to force its compliance rarely has a good ending, trying to force your husband to agree to counseling probably won't work. Using qualifiers when talking about the possibility of counseling may help your husband feel that he has not been cornered but has the freedom to consider the options.

Finding a Good Marriage Counselor

There are several things you can do to increase your chance of finding a high-quality marriage counselor. First, licenses matter—find a counselor who is a licensed professional. You will hear terms like licensed marriage and family therapist (LMFT), licensed psychologist, licensed professional counselor (LPC), and licensed social worker (LSW). Marriage counselors come from many different types of training and experience. It is important that the person you are working with has experience in marriage counseling, is licensed to do what he or she does, and has received training and supervision in marriage counseling. You can ask about their experience and training when you call to discuss treatment options with them.

Second, don't assume that you will work with the first counselor you see. Call several counselors, review their websites, and interview different therapists by phone. The process you are engaging in is important. Why not invest a little time and money up front to be sure you are working with the right person? You will probably not be looking for a psychiatrist, since they specialize in prescribing medicine, but you will find licensed psychologists, licensed marriage and family therapists, licensed professional counselors, and licensed social workers who can do the job. Psychologists have doctoral-level training and more years of supervised training than the others, who have master's level training. Choose a therapist whom you feel best matches your unique needs and personalities.

Third, and perhaps most important, you need to talk to people you know and get recommendations for counselors whom they can personally recommend. There is no stronger recommendation than that of clients who have already seen a psychologist or counselor. Licenses, experience, and training are extremely important, and interviewing different counselors is vital, but talking to people who personally recommend the individual with whom you are entrusting your marriage just makes good sense.

One last point to consider is utilizing a counselor who is a pastor, priest, or religious leader in your faith tradition. Although many of these folks do an excellent job counseling couples, you should know that many do not have formal training, supervision, or education in the area of marriage counseling. If you do choose to see a pastor or religious leader, I would highly recommend that you talk with them about their background and training in working with couples who are facing the type of challenges you are currently dealing with. This is especially true if you are seeking a counselor to work with the issues of power and control in marriage. As you no doubt realize after reading this far in the book, these issues are complex, long-standing, and challenging, and the counselor you work with should have experience working with these difficult issues.

What Marriage Counseling Is and Is Not

Marriage counselors treat the relationship, not the individual people in the relationship. When a husband or wife has a mental health disorder or other individual issue, these problems can't be treated in marriage counseling.

Marriage counseling is not appropriate when there has recently been, or there is a danger of, marital violence. When one or the other of you has threatened to harm the other physically, the conflicts that marriage counseling brings up can increase that danger. Before marriage counseling can occur, the potential violence has to be assessed by a certified domestic violence counselor (usually with the potentially violent person seeing that professional, and the other party seeing a victim's rights professional). Once both of those professionals have determined marriage counseling is safe, then it can begin.

When couples plan to divorce but decide to go to marriage counseling just to say they "gave it a shot," in most cases the counseling doesn't work well. If couples show evidence that one or both really don't want to be there, don't want to be married, and are strongly considering divorce, these issues need to be discussed first in counseling. I ask couples to agree to postpone divorce plans for at least three months, give their best effort to the counseling process, and then call the divorce attorneys if they choose.

Why I Believe Marriage Counseling Works

I truly believe that marriage counseling can help you and your husband deal with the power and control issues in your relationship. I have spent a lifetime working with couples, training counselors to work with couples, and studying the art of marriage counseling. I believe that if you follow the guidelines described in this chapter, you can find a counselor who is a good match for the two of you and your unique needs.

I am a huge fan of the counseling process, and there are three reasons why I strongly recommend marriage counseling for controlling husbands and their wives. First, I have seen husband after husband respond to the process in a positive manner. They often don't like what I have to say as a counselor, but they keep coming back and are more open to it as the process continues. Controlling husbands will often consider suggestions from an unbiased third party more easily than hearing them from their spouses.

Second, having someone in the room while you talk about these issues helps prevent the discussions from getting out of control. If your discussions tend to turn into arguments, a counselor can help serve as a moderator to make sure the process remains safe, respectful, and productive. This is especially important when one partner is more controlling than the other.

Third, and perhaps most importantly, it allows the counselor to see the controlling process in the relationship play out right there in the counseling room. The counselor is a witness—there is no "he said/she said" battle. Truth comes out, as all three parties know what actually happens, and the relationship is seen for what it truly is.

Marriage counseling can be an amazingly freeing experience for all involved, including the controlling husband. It provides the opportunity for different ways of communicating and relating to develop and lasting transformation to take place. I believe that you will find marriage counseling to be a safe place for both you and your husband to heal, to grow, and to change.

19

Our Story

The Happy Ending You Can Believe In

> Marriage is our last, best chance to grow up.
>
> Joseph Barth

May 24, 2014, was our twenty-eighth wedding anniversary. It's been a wild ride, and for all the ups and downs, there is no one I would rather have had with me than my amazing wife, Jan. I won't pretend that our marriage is perfect—far from it. We have struggles and challenges, but we have come a long, long way from the husband and wife we once were.

The process of writing this book has been a healing one for both Jan and me. These were not small wounds that we were reopening, and we knew it would be painful and difficult to share our story with the world. As the process comes to a close, this chapter, perhaps more than any other, should give you hope for the future of your own marriage.

Our marriage is stronger, deeper, more honest, more loving, and more committed than ever before. There is immense power in surviving the storm and coming out the other side. When we said, "I do," we didn't know each other that well. As you live together and face the challenges life brings, you begin to see the real person you married. It is then, and only then, that you can truly accept your partner as he or she is, faults and all, and understand what it means to devote your life to another.

Jan's Perspective

I asked Jan to share her thoughts about where we are in the marriage now. Her response, given below, provides a lot of wisdom and insight.

I feel that I have the freedom and support to be myself now. I would not have gone back to school or gotten my teaching license and two teaching positions without Ron's unconditional love, support, and belief in me. Now I can see Ron thinking before he responds, and he controls his anger almost all the time. I see him choosing my needs over his most of the time. If he is tired or overwhelmed, it is harder for him to do, but he is so much more open to listening when I tell him he is overreacting.

I can see the part I played in creating and allowing these patterns to be firmly established in the past. It will take time, patience, and true commitment to continue to work together to help each other live up to our potential. I know deep in my heart how hard Ron strives to be the husband I have always dreamed of. Sometimes I forget to recognize his achievements, especially when it is easier to concentrate on the negatives. I need to be intentional about remembering to say how much I appreciate his efforts in thinking of my needs before his own and including my wishes when he makes a decision.

Ron isn't perfect and he will always need to be very aware of his tendency to control me. He still makes comments that are too harsh or acts selfishly, but those times are much more rare now. The fun times and the joy are much more common. It is hard for me to trust that he will think of me first, and although the pressure to worry about his emotional response is much less, he can still get upset or frustrated. I have to realize that just because he does get upset, he has done so much better that I don't have to be afraid or hide things from him.

A couple of recent situations showed me how far we have come. On a recent vacation, Ron was so focused on making sure we did what I wanted that I didn't even realize we had skipped doing things he wanted to do. When we got home, it happened again, as we went to a movie I wanted to go to, and I didn't find out until later that he was going only for me. He has changed so much that I sometimes forget how selfish he used to be.

He is also no longer as jealous and possessive as he used to be. I can go anywhere I want, and he doesn't ask questions or try to find out what I have been doing. He trusts me so much more now and he no longer has all those controlling rules and expectations. It feels like I have been set free and I can be the woman and the wife I have always wanted to be.

My Perspective

As I consider the changes that have occurred in our marriage, I keep thinking about the four principles of Transformational Marriage. They are so central to what has changed in our marriage, it just makes sense to view our marriage through that lens. What follows are my impressions of how our marriage has changed in these four areas.

Praise

Praising each other took the least work in our marriage. We have always put a great deal of effort into building each other up, even during the darkest days. We made a habit from fairly early in our marriage of giving each other compliments and saying "I love you" on a regular basis. The challenge for us was that this was occurring in the shadow of my controlling behavior. My compliments didn't ring true for Jan when my behavior was not consistent with my words.

We have discovered that there are many benefits from complimenting each other. It's hard to be angry at someone who is giving you a compliment. People can often accept difficult feedback when it comes on the heels of hearing really positive things about themselves. It's like a safety net under a trapeze artist in a circus. Even if you fall, there's a soft place to land.

We still tell each other, every day, out loud, how much we love each other and the things that we appreciate about each other. The difference now is that the words mean immeasurably more because they are accompanied by actions that reinforce them. We have to be intentional about this; it is easy to become busy and not take the time to make it happen. Trust me—the time and energy invested will provide an outstanding return.

Hope

We have more hope than ever before. As you begin to implement the transformation that you have learned about in this book, you will become more and more hopeful. I think this is because when you are feeling helpless, hope is drained away. But when you can see changes taking place, there is hope. When Jan and I become frustrated with each other or disappoint each other, we no longer feel fearful that this is the best it can ever be. Now we *know* it can be better and we know how to make it better.

God has blessed us in so many ways. We have two amazing, wonderful sons who have become solid, mature young men. We have worked together for almost twenty-four of our twenty-eight years to provide a loving home with Christian values and we have learned that it takes the best efforts of both of us as a team to raise children in today's world. Whenever we face challenges or struggles, we look at our sons and feel proud of who they are and whatever part we played as a team in helping them mature.

Conflicts don't escalate like they used to. Jan still does things that frustrate me, and I make comments or act in ways that hurt Jan's feelings. The tendencies we both struggle with haven't disappeared, but we don't allow ourselves to get anywhere near going over the Falls as we used to. We have become quite good at preventing any conflict from getting worse, identifying where we are in the process, and focusing on how we are treating each other rather than the issue at hand.

These changes have created an extremely hopeful climate in our marriage. I wake up every day looking forward to time with Jan, to sharing life together, and to deepening our relationship. She no longer expects me to be "that controlling guy" but has begun to believe that I am capable of being the husband she deserves. We look toward the future with anticipation and joy, rather than fear and despair.

Forgiveness

Forgiveness has taken some work, mostly on Jan's part. She has had a lot more to forgive than I have. For many years, she struggled with believing that I could be the man she hoped I was. It was hard for her to focus on what I was doing well when there was still so much hurt from how I had treated her in the past.

As the years have gone by, and I have been able to consistently and repeatedly treat her in the ways she deserves, she has come to believe that I have truly changed. She now expects me to respect, honor, and support her. I know this because I see the surprise in her eyes now when I am not at my best, as she has come to expect me to put her needs before my own.

In our marriage, forgiveness is intricately tied to selflessness. When I am focusing on what Jan needs, thinking about her feelings and how she will hear things I say, it becomes unlikely that I will do something that requires her forgiveness. We both try hard to see what happens during the day through a wider lens of the overall way we are treating each other.

For me, it's like baseball. If Jan has been batting around .800 and almost always considering my feelings, thinking about my needs, and respecting and honoring me, why on earth would I want to hold the one time she doesn't do that against her? It wouldn't make sense.

My wife is an inherently good person; she radiates love, warmth, and kindness to everyone she meets. When I look at the beautiful woman God saw fit to create and allow me to share my life with, forgiveness becomes easy. When you are the one who has wronged the other in the relationship, it's your partner who has to bear the cross of forgiveness. Jan has found it in her heart to put the past behind her and move forward, and I will be forever grateful to her for the gift of her forgiveness.

Selflessness

Selflessness was the key that unlocked every other door in our marriage. When I was busy controlling people every chance I got, I had no idea that thinking of other people's needs before my own could actually be enjoyable. I operated under the assumption that there could be no better feeling than protecting myself from the perceived fears and dangers that seemed to be all around me. It never occurred to me that I could experience joy and peace, let alone comfort and security, through focusing on others' needs before my own.

As I have made this transformation, which continues on a daily basis, I am discovering why Jan always seems so happy when making others happy. I have heard people who desire to serve others called a variety of negative names: codependent, no backbone, weak, doormat. I used to accept these descriptions as truth, assuming that fighting for your own needs was what *strong* people did.

My wife has taught me that serving others is what makes us truly human. So much of our society focuses on getting money, power, sex, and control, but these things do not make us happy, joyful, peaceful, and content. Jan has shown me that there is actually great freedom and joy in caring for others' needs before my own.

If relationships are nurtured under the warm sunshine of servanthood and selflessness, everything else falls into place. For me, this was the most important factor in transforming my thoughts, my actions, and my marriage.

Success Breeds Success

One of the biggest lessons I have learned on our journey is that success breeds success. Praise is infectious; building each other up with compliments and warmth comes back to you in waves from your partner. The more we hope, the more hopeful we become. The more we forgive each other, the easier forgiveness becomes. As selflessness becomes a way of life for us, it takes less and less effort to focus on each other. Success breeds success in all these areas.

All of these principles work together to create transformation in your marriage. When you praise each other, you become more hopeful about the future of your marriage. When you act in selfless ways, it becomes easier to forgive each other for the inevitable failures. People who have hope in the future of their relationship are more likely to be forgiving. When partners praise each other, they become selfless in the very act of praising the other. It all ties together.

We Never Marry the Person We Marry

The moment you said, "I do," your husband or wife became a different person. But that shouldn't be a surprise to you—your partner has been growing and changing since the day he or she was born. The question is: Will your love and acceptance of your spouse continue to grow also? For a marriage to flourish, you have to learn to accept, appreciate, and respect these changes. At the same time, you have to set boundaries and maintain expectations that lead to your being treated with that same acceptance, appreciation, and respect.

Since we never marry the person we marry, there may have been promises made on your wedding day that have not been kept, and those failures need to be forgiven. Some of your hopes and dreams may not have come true. Perhaps you have each become selfish in many ways and have forgotten to pay attention to all the wonderful qualities about your mate. These are the areas where transformation must occur.

You have now learned the skills that can transform your marriage. You have the ability to see what is happening, to get out of the river before you go over the Falls, and to live differently. It is time to recommit to the person you love, with all his or her flaws. It may even be time to renew your wedding vows and make a firm commitment to this "new" person you find yourself married to. You deserve to be loved, honored, and respected, and so does your spouse.

It is my sincere hope that our story has touched you, the person you are sharing your life with, and your relationship in meaningful ways. This project really was a labor of love. If our story has somehow encouraged you, motivated you, or transformed you—if your marriage becomes stronger, warmer, more loving, more intimate, or just better—for that I am truly thankful.

Your marriage is exactly that—your marriage. What happens now is up to you and the one you love. Choose to think of the other before yourself. Choose to be honest with each other. Choose to love, honor, and respect the person you have decided to spend your life with. Become the person you have always known you were capable of being, and help your partner do the same. Praise, hope, forgive, serve, love, and transform your marriage.

Notes

Chapter 1 Why This Book Is for You

1. Centers for Disease Control and Prevention, "Births, Marriages, Divorces, and Deaths: Provisional Data for 2009," http://www.cdc.gov/nchs/data/nvsr58/nvsr58_25.pdf.

2. Willard F. Harley, Jr., *Effective Marriage Counseling* (Grand Rapids: Revell, 2010), 93.

3. Jean Twenge, "Birth Cohort Increases in Narcissistic Personality Traits among American College Students, 1982–2009," *Social Psychological and Personality Science*, January 1, 2010, 99–106.

Chapter 4 The Alpha Male Problem

1. David Mech, "Alpha Status, Dominance, and Division of Labor in Wolf Packs," *Canadian Journal of Zoology* 77 (1999): 1196–1203.

2. Vince Lombardi, "Famous Quotes," http://www.vincelombardi.com.

3. Rod Olson, *The Legacy Builder* (Colorado Springs: David C Cook, 2013), 124–26.

4. Ryan Hedstrom and Daniel Gould, "Research in Youth Sports: Critical Issues Status—White Paper Summaries of the Existing Literature," Institute for the Study of Youth Sports, November 1, 2004, 21–24.

Chapter 5 The Three Keys to Control

1. Lundy Bancroft, *Why Does He Do That?* (London: Penguin, 2002), 3.

2. National Institute of Justice, "Full Report of the Prevalence, Incidence, and Consequences of Violence against Women: Findings from the National Violence against Women Survey," http://www.ojp.usdoj.gov/nij/pubs-sum/183781.htm.

3. Gary Chapman, *Desperate Marriages* (Chicago: Northfield, 2008), 121.

4. Ibid., 87–88.

5. Gary and Carrie Oliver, "Cultivating Healthy Anger in Your Marriage," in David Stoop and Jan Stoop, eds., *The Complete Marriage Book: Practical Help from Leading Experts* (Grand Rapids: Revell, 2002), 206–17.

6. Dorothy McCoy, *The Manipulative Man* (Avon, MA: Adams Media, 2006), 1–3.

7. Patricia Evans, *Controlling People* (Avon, MA: Adams Media, 2002), 153–60.

Chapter 6 The Three Questions Wives Ask Most

1. George Barna, "How America's Faith Has Changed Since 9/11," http://www
.barna.org/barna-update/article/5-barna-update/63-how-americas-faith-has-
changed-since-9-11.

2. Bobbi Carothers and Harry Reis, "Men and Women Are from Earth: Examining the Latent Structure of Gender," *Journal of Personality and Social Psychology*,
October 22, 2012, 1–23.

3. Patricia Evans, *The Verbally Abusive Man: Can He Change?* (Avon, MA:
Adams, 2006).

Chapter 9: Storm Front 2

1. Aaron Beck, *Cognitive Therapy of Personality Disorders*, 2nd ed. (New
York: Guilford, 2007), 275.

2. Martin Seligman and Steven Maier, "The Alleviation of Learned Helplessness in Dogs," *Journal of Abnormal Psychology* 73 (1968): 256–62.

Chapter 10 Storm Front 3

1. Craig Blomberg, personal communication, February 2013.

2. William Spencer et al., *Marriage at the Crossroads: Couples in Conversation about Discipleship, Gender Roles, Decision Making, and Intimacy* (Downers
Grove, IL: IVP Academic, 2009), 57–94.

3. Henry Cloud and John Townsend, *Boundaries* (Grand Rapids: Zondervan,
1992), 150–66.

4. Ibid., 161.

5. Craig Blomberg, "Craig Blomberg Blog," denverseminary.edu, http://
www.denverseminary.edu/craig-blombergs-blog-new-testament-musings/making
-marriage-work/.

Chapter 11 Going over Niagara Falls

1. William Fleeman, "Niagara Falls Metaphor Video Description," Pathways
to Peace, http://www.cecomet.net/~insite/ptp/videodesc.html.

2. Chapman, *Desperate Marriages*, 126.

3. Ibid., 128.

Chapter 13 Transforming Your Marriage for a Lifetime

1. Timothy Keller, *The Meaning of Marriage* (New York: Dutton, 2011), 29.

2. "Online Dating Statistics," http://www.statisticbrain.com/online-dating
-statistics.

3. Pamela Paul, *The Starter Marriage and the Future of Matrimony* (New
York: Villard, 2002), 3–6.

4. Harville Hendrix and Helen Hunt, *Getting the Love You Want: A Guide for
Couples,* 20th anniv. ed. (New York: Henry Holt, 2007), 247–84.

Chapter 14 Praising Each Other

1. John Gottman and Robert Levenson, "A Two-Factor Model for Predicting When a Couple Will Divorce: Exploratory Analyses Using 14-Year Longitudinal Data," *Family Process* 41(2002): 83–96.

2. Harley, *Effective Marriage* Counseling, 15.

3. Jack Balswick and Judith Balswick, *A Model for Marriage: Covenant, Grace, Empowerment, and Intimacy* (Downers Grove, IL: InterVarsity, 2006), 63–72.

4. John Gottman, *The Seven Principles for Making Marriage Work* (New York: Three Rivers Press, 2000), 27–34.

5. Stephen Kendrick and Alex Kendrick, *The Love Dare* (Nashville: B & H Books, 2008).

Chapter 15 Finding Hope in Each Other

1. Everett Worthington, *Hope-Focused Marriage Counseling: A Guide to Brief Therapy* (Downers Grove, IL: IVP Academic, 2005).

Chapter 16 Forgiving Each Other

1. Alex Harris et al., "Effects of a Group Forgiveness Intervention on Forgiveness, Perceived Stress and Trait Anger: A Randomized Trial," *Journal of Clinical Psychology* 62 (2006): 715–33.

2. Frank Fincham, Steven Beach, and Joanne Davila, "Longitudinal Relations between Forgiveness and Conflict Resolution in Marriage," *Journal of Family Psychology* 21 (2007): 542–45.

3. Peter Wason, "On the Failure to Eliminate Hypotheses in a Conceptual Task," *Quarterly Journal of Experimental Psychology* 12 (1960): 129–40.

4. Robert Merton, "The Self-Fulfilling Prophecy," *Antioch Review* 8 (1948): 193–210.

5. Tim and Julie Clinton, "Breaking the Cycle of Conflict," in Stoop, *The Complete Marriage Book*, 185.

6. Craig Blomberg, "On Building and Breaking Barriers: Forgiveness, Salvation, and Christian Counseling with Special Reference to Matthew 18:15–35," *Journal of Psychology and Christianity* 25 (2006): 137–54.

Chapter 17 Serving Each Other

1. Keller, *The Meaning of Marriage*, 56–57.

2. C. S. Lewis, *Mere Christianity* (New York: MacMillan, 1952), 99.

3. Ibid., 100.

Dr. Ron Welch (PsyD, Central Michigan University) serves on the faculty of Denver Seminary. Welch has over twenty years of experience in clinical psychology and has extensive experience working with couples and men with narcissistic and antisocial personality styles. He has developed the Transformational Marriage™ approach, which helps couples through counseling, seminars, and publications. He and his wife, Jan, have walked the road of a controlling marriage personally and live in Colorado.

For more information about the

Transformational Marriage™

approach developed by

Dr. Ron Welch,

visit Transformational-Marriage.com or email
help@transformational-marriage.com

• • • • • • • • • • • • • • •

Transformational Marriage™
Counseling & Seminars
Re Think • Re Build • Re Love

The best book on marriage is now
better than ever!

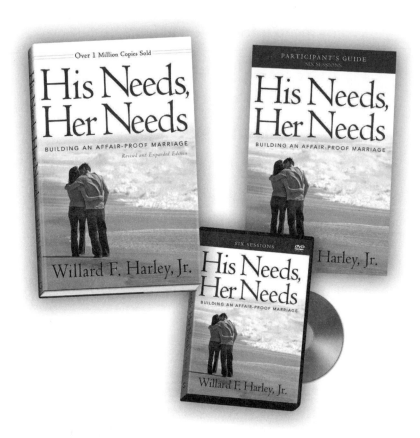

For over twenty-five years, *His Needs, Her Needs* has been transforming marriages all over the world. Now this life-changing book is the basis for an interactive six-week DVD study designed for use in couples' small groups or retreats, in premarital counseling sessions, or by individual couples.

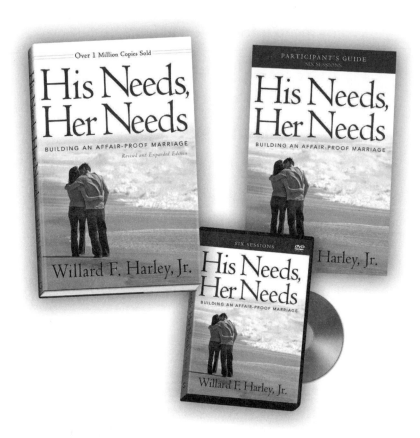

Ɍ Revell
a division of Baker Publishing Group
www.RevellBooks.com

Available Wherever Books Are Sold
Also Available in Ebook Format

Have a New Husband by Friday?
Is that even possible?

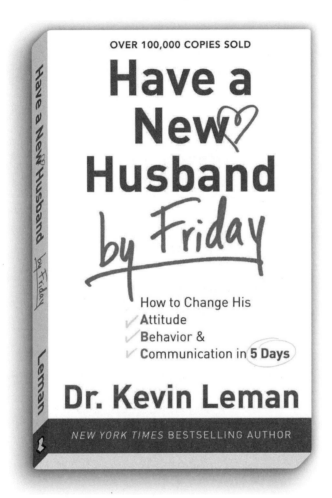

Dr. Kevin Leman says it is. The *New York Times* bestselling author and relationship expert shows you how with his easy and accessible principles.

Ꝝ Revell
a division of Baker Publishing Group
www.RevellBooks.com

Be the First to Hear about Other New Books from REVELL!

Sign up for announcements about new and upcoming titles at

RevellBooks.com/SignUp

Don't miss out on our great reads!

Revell

a division of Baker Publishing Group
www.RevellBooks.com